THE COWARD
ROB FORD

Also by Nicholas Osborn

THE COWARD ROB FORD

Bullets Legend
Book 1

NICHOLAS OSBORN

WOLFPACK
PUBLISHING
— EST 2013 —

The Coward Rob Ford
Paperback Edition
Copyright © 2025 by Nicholas Osborn

Wolfpack Publishing
1707 E. Diana Street
Tampa, Florida 33610

www.wolfpackpublishing.com

Paperback ISBN 979-8-89567-421-5
Ebook ISBN 979-8-89567-420-8

THE COWARD
ROB FORD

Chapter 1

Robbie B. Ford has always been a no-good coward.

Since being delivered into this wretched world, his belly had become indistinguishable

from the golden Texas sun shining upon his hurry down the worst paths life had to offer. Some men of the world find strength in their principles, hold firm to what is right, and remain steadfast in their pursuit of the most just actions. The man who preferred to simply be called Rob wasn't one of them. Cowardice had reared its ugly face more often than not for most of his life. When he was no taller than a doorknob, he didn't really give it much thought, but as he grew older, he knew there was no getting rid of that all too familiar urge deep down in the pit of his stomach.

His dad always said he gave him that cursed name for a reason, said that it was just a feeling he had when he held him as a crying newborn. Being completely honest with himself, Rob didn't know what that even meant. Even so, whether he wanted it or not, he'd earned his namesake through the years by doing what all cowards do best—avoiding, procrastinating, and most importantly, running.

That's exactly what he was doing when he sent two of his least favorite acquaintances and work associates into a home hidden in the trees beneath the moonlight to snag whatever they could while he went to work. He was in the cattle business, for lack of a better description, despite the fact that he didn't actually own any cattle. He was a man who delivered as many head of cattle as he could get his hands on, rolling the dice every time he got on the back of a horse and pocketing a portion of the proceeds that came as a result, only after the notorious Bossman got his cut, of course. He was in charge of leading a crew not too unlike a batch of rowdy cowboys right off the frontier, and tonight, they were loading up about sixty pairs across a whole fleet of gooseneck trailers. It was an easy gig. Most people don't even realize cattle rustling could still earn a living in this day and age. He didn't need much, considering most of his wages were confiscated toward an outstanding debt he was still working on paying off, but work was steady. Even then, a side income never hurt no one. Stealing cattle was one thing, but going inside someone's home in the hopes of an unspoken bonus was something else entirely.

"It's right through them woods, that way," said Rob with a finger pointed in the opposite direction he was headed himself. "Y'all'll be fine as long as you don't jack around too much. Get back here when you find something worth finding."

"Who lives there again?" Hicks asked, his shaggy beard and backward baseball cap stained in oil doing their best to hide his concern.

The partner in crime standing next to Hicks, far

from the brains of the duo, was a man who willingly went by the name of Hogtie. He'd earned the moniker a few years back from the local police department after an incident which left half a dozen people hogtied in a gas station parking lot. The man didn't know a heifer from a steer, but even Rob knew it wasn't a bad thing to have a man who could pull something like that off when it was needed. Hogtie wasn't a man of many words, so neither Hicks nor Rob were surprised when he answered with only a blank stare.

"Hogtie here doesn't think it matters," said Rob. "He's right, too. It don't."

"Just don't want to get my ass shot is all."

"It's the middle of the night, Hicks."

"That's my point. Why don't *you* go?"

Rob took a step forward but stopped himself before going any further. "You saying you want my job? You can tell the Bossman why it's you pulling down that long driveway in a few hours for the drop off when he's expecting me, then. Don't bother me none."

"I didn't say that."

Hogtie nudged Hicks, still refusing to say anything.

"Listen to your buddy," said Rob. "If it makes you feel any better, we're about a dozen head shy of what we were told would be here, so whatever you're about to get into is gonna be a hell of a lot easier than what's waiting on me."

"It don't."

"Go on, before it's too late," Rob's words came, as he was already scurrying away without looking back, leaving the two accomplices behind, wondering what just happened.

Hicks turned to leave, and Hogtie followed right

3

behind. They had been working together as trailer hands, pushing and sorting cattle for the last couple of years, longer than their new crew leader had been with the outfit. They'd been around a long time, but not long enough to know who Rob really was. Hicks didn't know he followed a coward, and Hogtie just didn't care one way or another. They only considered Rob to be a necessary evil for their own ambitions.

"You really like putting up with him?" Hicks was heated.

The question still wasn't important enough to warrant a response from Hogtie.

"I think he just wants to screw with us," Hicks continued. "Or maybe he's tryin' to see how much we're gonna put up with. You know, like puttin' us under the gun type of thing? It might mean we're gonna get promoted soon. Hate to be the ones to tell 'em, but that ain't what we're after, is it buddy?"

This time, Hogtie let out a grunt. It came from deep in his gut and caused his shoulders to twitch beneath a faded flannel button-down with only half of its buttons remaining.

"Besides, how long do they think we're gonna get away with this in a county so small? Word gets around Harrison County, and there are only so many old men with too many cows around. Greener pastures are out there, buddy. We just gotta find 'em."

Hicks and Hogtie made no effort to conceal their trek through the dense woods filled with yaupon limbs slapping their faces and spiderwebs blocking their path. Greenbriar thorns threatened to trip them up with each step, cicadas blasted their ears, and muggy humidity filled their lungs. Streaks of moonlight filtered through the pines and bald cypress overhead, providing barely enough light to see their way forward. Every reason nature could muster to force the two into moving in silence was ignored completely by the two would-be thieves in the night.

"What do ya think we'll find in there, anyway?" Hicks continued his rambling. "Remember that place off of 154 a while back? Who carries around a $10,000 wad of cash? If you ask me, that man wanted to get robbed."

Hogtie turned to look at Hicks. His empty glare did all the talking, as it normally did with miraculous specificity.

"Yeah, I'm not sure either," said Hicks. "I do know one thing, we're puttin' a little extra in our pocket this time. We've damn sure earned it."

Their walk carried on for more than an hour, through a barbed wire fence, and across a creek that soaked their boots right down to their socks. They pushed forward regardless, with Rob's parting wisdom echoing in their thoughts. Finding something worth finding wasn't always as easy as it sounded. They all spoke the same language, though. No matter what happened, if their wallets didn't get a little bit thicker after the job, it was a failure.

To say Hicks gave up on the pointless conversation would be an outright lie. He was a nervous talker, and their hike through the woods gave him more than enough time to work his way through every thought that entered his head. This was annoying to pretty much everyone except Hogtie. Most of the guys they ran with said Hogtie just liked listening to him, and that was fine by him.

"Gotta be around here somewhere."

Before the words had escaped his lips, Hicks realized the shadowy structure rising in the

distance surrounded by the silhouettes of towering trees all around. Traces of moonlight danced off hidden leaves in the night, hinting at a path forward through the brush. It didn't take long to see the home begin to take shape ahead of them. Its stone chimney attached to the side of the two-story home rose into the air with nearly invisible smoke billowing from the top. A driveway formed beneath their feet within the next few minutes, guiding the rest of their way inside.

Finding a window to break into was easy enough, and even then, Hicks kept the pointless conversation flowing. This time, instead of damn near hollering at Hogtie, his voice had dropped to a whisper.

"We get in and out, just like last time. You find the wallets, I'll find the safe," said Hicks, before Hogtie yanked open the window just enough to allow them both to crawl inside. Before Hogtie could push his head inside the home, Hicks pulled him back. "Anything goes wrong, we meet here and get the hell outta' Dodge. Okay?"

Hogtie shrugged his shoulders and leaped inside. Hicks followed soon after. The first thing he saw when he landed inside the expansive home was a family portrait with five people huddled around a gravesite with the word *Hunter* etched into the frame. Hicks didn't think anything of it. He pushed forward into the home, hiding his sopping wet boots, hitting the hardwood floors as best he could.

Hogtie broke off toward the front door, and Hicks did his best to find a closet. They usually only had minutes at best to sort through a home before things turned south. This made it particularly unusual when Hicks heard a commotion from upstairs, no more than fifteen seconds after they had broken in. His heart rate jumped in response, forcing him to take a deep breath and get his bearings back.

There was no way anyone had already caught onto them. He was just being dramatic, and he knew that. He had a tendency to overreact, and this case was surely no different. That's what he was telling himself over and over again as he made his way further into the home. When the first door he wanted to peek behind creaked open, his worst fears immediately became a nightmare unfolding around him.

Bam.

Hicks didn't see the bullet slam into the back of Hogtie's head. All he saw was a black spray of blood against the wall, almost indistinguishable in the darkness. Almost. What Hicks had witnessed sent a shiver down his spine that begged to crawl out of his lungs in an uncontrollable scream. Just like that, Hogtie was dead, twitching on the floor. His boots tapping against the hardwood floors would be burned into his memory for as long as he lived.

"Hogtie!"

It was all he could let out before his thoughtless scramble carried him in the other direction. He pushed open the door that he was only going to glance behind and rushed inside. What he found was a clutter that couldn't be described. Stacks of aging books, letters, and loose documents were piled to the ceiling, falling over suitcases and cardboard boxes tossed haphazardly throughout the room. There were glass cases packed full of worn firearms and swords, antique artwork and sculptures, and for an inexplicable reason, more loose pages with cursive scribbles made with ink from ages ago. It was the kind of room that belonged to a collector, or a hoarder, but it was undeniably one that any history buff could easily appreciate. To Hicks, however, it was without a doubt the last place he wanted to die in.

The door slammed shut behind him with a *thud* so loud he knew it had to have given away where he was hiding. The nightmare he'd found himself in continued when a bullet tore through the door and lodged into a wall on the other side of the room. Hicks was staring down his own death, unable to escape the very fate that had befallen his closest friend, Hogtie.

His chest heaved up and down in frantic breaths as he desperately searched for a way out of the room. Bookshelves lined the walls, each one more crammed full of books than the last. On the other side of a desk, lost in the sea of folders and paperwork scattered around—just around the corner of a pile of boxes stacked as tall as Hicks—was the answer to all of his problems. It was a glimpse of hope amid complete despair, a chance given when there was none left to be had. It was a door.

All he had to do was get to it alive. Hicks didn't think well under duress, and since it was the first time he'd actually been shot at, he'd have been lucky if he remembered his own name. When he felt the weight on his hip pressing into him as he sat crouched against the door, he could have fallen over for feeling so damn stupid.

Hicks had carried his 9mm G19 loaded with 147-grain hollow points to the fight, and those sixteen rounds would sure go a long way for him in the situation he'd found himself in. It took only a split second to draw the polymer handgun from his waistband, aim it at the door he was hiding behind, and squeeze the trigger.

Bam. Bam. Bam. Bam.

He kept squeezing the trigger, over and over again. After the first seven shots, he closed his eyes and began to yell any obscenity he could think of. He fired off round after round, each one blasting only a few inches from his face, sending splintered wood chips flying in the air. Every bullet made him feel just a little bit safer, so he kept firing.

Bam. Bam. Bam. Bam.

It wasn't until he was forced to take another breath that he realized he had forgotten to keep count of his bullets. Was he at thirteen now? He knew there were at least two more rounds in the magazine for sure, so he allowed himself to squeeze the trigger one more time for good measure. To his terror, the slide of the G19 locked back. He was out of ammo.

Smoke filled his nostrils, carrying whiffs of burned gunpowder strong enough to make him wince. There was a dim bulb tucked away in the corner of the room, letting shadows stretch out across everything stuffed inside, making him feel more alone than ever. The silence that followed after his sporadic unloading of the magazine fell heavy over Hicks. He should have been reloading. He should have been doing everything he could to get back in the fight he never wanted to be in. There was only one problem.

He forgot his spare magazine in the truck.

Frozen in fear, Hicks felt his stomach sink to the

floor when he realized what he'd done. His fingers trembled, his breathing was frantic, and his heart felt like it was going to beat right out of his chest. The holes in the door he was propped against let in a faint trace of air conditioning that brushed against his face, making him think someone was trying to sneak in.

Hicks felt his body scramble to his feet. He couldn't think straight, much less keep his

composure to move through the stacks of boxes without falling on his face. The first time he hit the floor, he didn't even think about picking himself up. He just did it. The fear of what was surely right behind him sent him sprinting deeper into the room, stepping on torn pages and leaving a trail of destruction behind him.

The next time he hit the floor, his face landed on a black leather notebook, cracked and wrinkled from age. Its yellowed pages and worn edges made it seem mundane, but there was something about it that spoke to Hicks, like a whisper in a dream. In a room packed full of some of history's hardest antiquities to find, the man who had been sent to find something worth finding made his choice right then and there.

Up on his feet again, he put one still-soaking-wet boot in front of the other, refusing to so much as glance at anything other than the door no more than a few feet away from him. Salvation was on the other side. All he had to do was reach it. Hicks did his best not to think of his best friend lying dead somewhere in the house, and how there would be no salvation for Hogtie. He had to get out. The notebook he'd stolen was the last thing on his mind, but it at least meant he'd gained something after giving so much.

The horrifyingly familiar creaking of a door

swinging open made Hicks feel as though he was going to hurl. There was a bullet coming for his head any second, he just knew it. His hand finally grasped the knob and twisted so hard he damn near ripped it off the door. On the other side was a hallway, far from the clean escape he'd wished so desperately to find. Hicks was left with no choice but to make a run for it anyway.

Whether it was the folly of man or his own stupidity, he was unable to suppress his own curiosity about who was shooting at him. For reasons he couldn't believe himself, he sacrificed a crucial split second to turn his head for a glimpse at who was coming after him. He saw only sweeping black hair falling down the back of a woman holding a revolver outstretched in one arm. Her eyes were as black as the shadows Hicks was running from. Her glare pierced his very soul. Before he could look away, he saw the fires of hell escape from the end of the revolver's barrel. Its flame reached toward him, blinding in the darkness, ringing his ears with its scream.

He expected searing pain, or worse, the emptiness of death to creep over his body when the bullet was fired. Glass shattering ahead of him gave him the first glimmer of hope since he saw what happened to Hogtie, though. He was sprinting as fast as his adrenaline-fueled legs would allow. When he tumbled through the window at the end of the hallway, the gash in his forearm and blood streaming down his face somehow felt more freeing than anything else. Hicks' heart jumped at the open race to the wood line in the distance, the sheer thought of survival sending him fleeing from the home he never should have entered.

The weight of the leather notebook tucked in his

back pocket reminded him of the words of his boss, Rob, as he ran away into the trees, *Find something worth finding.*

After what he'd seen in the house, he was sure he'd done just that.

Chapter 2

There was once a day when barbed wire stood as the largest threat to rustlers hoping to pull one over on cattlemen devoting their blood, sweat, and tears to the frontier.

These days, there are protections that couldn't even be imagined by the most infamous of thieves in the Wild West. Herd management technology had long joined the 21st century, ushering in an age where stealing cattle was as unheard of as charges for horse theft. These types of things just didn't happen anymore. From electronic identification devices to networks of registration, tracing ownership and lineage for generations, it was almost impossible to misplace cattle on a large scale. Almost.

The trail of taillights from half a dozen twenty-four-foot stainless gooseneck trailers lining the dirt driveway were unmistakable. Each one with a side ramp splayed open into the pasture that extended out into the night. There were calls coming from the distance, hollers and bellowing that sounded like thunder rolling in. The red glow of the taillights were their finish line, and the race that was unfolding was one that had been run for many years.

"Yah!"

"Get!"

"Yip! Yip!"

"Go on, ya sons of bitches!"

A torrent of hooves and screams from those approaching through the darkness rose into the air without remorse. They were not hiding what was taking place. They were not shying away from what was happening. They were modern-day cattle rustlers, and for a moment, their task was no different than that undertaken by those burdened by the same calling in the 1800s. As the herd approached, pushed onward by the mounted cowboys following closely behind, the trailers waited stoically for what was about to happen.

To watch the cowboys of today at work was no different than analyzing the pen of an artist. Every swoop, every straight line, every stray scribble, all placed with precision and grace to form something aimed only at attracting the lingering gaze of any passerby. These were the actions of sorting, pushing, and leading done by the men and their trusted horses. They worked in unison, never missing a beat, communicating through unspoken subtleties and a language spoken only by those fortunate enough to have been taught it by their elders.

"Y'all better be ready!" A booming voice carried out of the tree line before anything else was visible. "We're comin' in hot!"

"Yip! Yip!" The cries continued out.

"Go! Go! Go!"

Right on cue, each of the trailers produced a man

in a cowboy hat who ran down the ramp with their arms held wide to plant their boots in the mud even wider. They joined the sweeping array of cowboys pushing a herd upward to sixty head at a pace few could dare keep up with. To the untrained eye, it would have been majestic, but to those who knew what was happening in the middle of the night, there was only one way to describe it—illegal.

With the market experiencing record highs in the area and showing no signs of slowing down, cow-calf pairs closing in on a thousand pounds were pushing three thousand dollars a pop. That meant if they did their homework right, this job should pull close to two hundred thousand dollars in market value. Not too bad for one night's work.

These were the same numbers floating through Rob's head as he rode alongside the team of cowboys he most often referred to as his outfit. He was in his late twenties, but looked like he turned forty yesterday. His scruffy chin, crow's feet, and deep-set black eyes were almost impossible to make out beneath of wide-brimmed 10X black felt cowboy hat that hadn't seen a brush in too many years. He wore a mahogany waxed canvas jacket and starched denim over manure-stained leather square-toe boots.

He'd been trusted to lead the group, for better or worse. He may have been a lowly man on the totem pole when it came to who was making the decisions, but when it came time to carry them out, he was the guy Bossman would call on. Even though he hadn't actually met the man everyone referred to as *Bossman*, he knew enough about him to answer the phone when his name came across his phone. Every time he got a phone call from him, Rob made himself, and everyone around him, just a little bit richer.

Tonight would be no different, from the looks of it. The three cowboys he was with and the drivers who'd hauled the trailers for them were operating like a well-oiled machine, just the way he'd drawn it up. Their trick was to be quick, to get in and out before anyone had a chance to catch on. By the time the old ranchers realized they'd been had, their cattle were already part of a system designed to make them disappear into an industry not nearly enough people were paying attention to.

This kind of business wasn't foolproof, but it was damn sure steady. There was no shortage of cattle around them, and because the days of the thousand-acre ranches led by the most influential people in town had long gone, there was also no shortage of men with too few resources to fight them. The men who remained were already barely hanging on as it was. It would take a man of a certain caliber to do what was required and steal their last chance to hope.

It just so happened that Rob was that man.

It wasn't like he dreamed of riding horseback through the night to steal a bunch of cattle from poor old men and their families when he was growing up. He was driven to such means as most men are, through an upbringing lacking in moral fiber and a world far crueler to him than it would ever be to those he knew. This kind of pressure had created some of the world's best men, but also some of the worst.

By the time Rob and his outfit had reached the line of trailers, the drivers were wielding paddles, ready to sort on the move and in a hurry. They maneuvered their horses into a half circle alongside the herd and slowed the pace to a trot. These were Brangus crosses, black-hided cattle with generations of docility bred into them. Moving and sorting were easier with genetics like this, and Rob's men put it to use.

One by one, the drivers stepped headfirst into the oncoming herd, joined immediately by a cowboy cutting less than a dozen pairs off. Their hooves hitting the ramps shook and rattled the first trailer and then the second. Each driver slammed the ramp shut, locked the door, then gave the trailer a ritualistic hard-handed slap before hurrying around to the other side to hop in the truck.

Without saying a word, the cowboys circled back to the herd, falling in line to be the next to cut off another dozen or so pairs from the herd. Each trailer reached its full capacity in moments before the next one in line was ready to load. When the last batch of pairs ran up the final ramp and the clanking of metal gates and chains came to a stop, the fleet of trailers sat waiting for the word to move, a word which could only come from Rob.

Instead of sending the trailers on their way or rounding up the outfit for a final word before leaving the scene of the crime, Rob knew there was unfinished business with the ones who were told to collect on their bonuses. There wasn't much time to kill before he'd be forced to do something no one wanted to do, so he killed what he could in the only way he knew. Still mounted on the same old mare he rode time and time again, Rob gripped onto the reins with one hand to gently come to a stop before he took a deep breath and began to sing.

Well I hired out to Diamond Joe, boys.

I did offer him my hand.
And he gave me a string of horses
so old they could not stand.
Well I liked to have died of hunger.
He did mistreat me so.
I never earned a dollar,
in the pay of Diamond Joe.

His voice carried across the cold night air with an emotional twang that men swarm to Nashville every year in an attempt to recreate. It was a jarring moment of unexpected placidness, set against a backdrop of dozens of cattle slamming back and forth in their aluminum trailers. For the cowboys who had worked with him before, it was a welcome return to form and a sign that the work was reaching its end. For the drivers who were still waiting on a chance to do their job, it was an unwelcome distraction.

He crooned back and forth in his saddle as he rode, missing only a guitar to pluck as the song poured out of him. He motioned his horse gently over to the last trailer in line and slowed his gait before falling silent at last. Rob had been taught tricks of the trade through his time spent as *an ass in the saddle*, but it didn't take much brains to know not to trust a headcount he didn't do himself. If it was worth asking someone else what the count was, it was worth doing it yourself.

He rode carefully next to each trailer, his mouth just barely moving as he kept a tediously strict number climbing higher and higher in his head. Rob may have been a coward for most of his life, but that didn't mean he was stupid. He knew better than anyone that the trick to staying ahead in this world, and staying alive around the wrong type of people, was to do what you say you're going to do. He said he'd bring in the new herd Coleman Ranch leased on the property not too far from Caddo Lake, so that's what he was going to do.

"Sixty-five," he finally spoke up. "It ain't quite six dozen pairs like we were promised, but it ain't too far off either."

"Still a pretty penny," a redheaded cowboy named Sam Simpson rode up closer to comment. He was still in his twenties and held an unexplained vendetta against most forms of personal hygiene, making him all too easy to sniff out of a crowd. "That is what we're after, right?"

"You know something, Sam?" Another of Rob's outfit came riding up. His name was Cliff Jackson, and there was really only one way to describe him—an asshole. "After riding with you for one damn night, I think it's safe to say the only thing any of us are after is a godforsaken bar of soap."

"I'd give just about anything to see that horse of yours give one good go at kicking you right in the head, you son of a bitch."

"My horse likes me," said Cliff. "You sittin' so close to that poor thing's nose is nothing short of animal abuse, though. Can't imagine what your horse thinks of your nasty, smellin' ass."

"Both of you," Rob interjected. "Give the word."

"What about Hicks and Hogtie?" Sam asked.

"They know the deal."

Without another word, Sam and Cliff rode off beneath the stars, drenched in a red light from the trailers waiting behind diesels roaring at a standstill. Rob listened to the barking of orders and the inevitable revving of motors that signaled the departure of the pairs they'd just loaded. One by one, each of the six twenty-four-foot trailers escaped down the dirt road leading to the pasture they'd found themselves in. All Rob could do was enjoy the peaceful hum of the cicadas in the distance and reflect on the night's work.

The Coleman Ranch was considered untouchable to anyone who knew the last name. They ran fifteen hundred head of cattle on a bad day and had a penchant for swallowing up any land that came up for sale in a hundred-mile radius. There were Colemans running the local tack supply store, holding chairs on the city council, and policing the county. There was even a Sheriff Coleman roaming around and signs on every business corner in red, white, and blue colors reading, *Vote for Mayor Coleman.*

Despite all of the red flags, Rob had been picking off scraps of their herd for the last couple of months. Every time their name was brought up, he'd fought against it, but at the end of the day, it wasn't his decision. He was still in a place where he had no choice but to do as he was told. As he watched the trailers pull away with yet another load of pairs from the Coleman Ranch, he knew two things were holding true—his luck would hold for one more night, and it was one day closer to giving out.

The rustling of yaupons twenty feet behind where Rob sat deep in the saddle without moving, stirred him from his introspection. Any other night, he would've assumed it was a hog or even a raccoon up to no good, but he knew that wasn't the case. There was a reason he sent Hicks and Hogtie to break into a stranger's home.

"We almost left y'all behind," Rob spoke without turning his head.

"Sir," a shaky voice came from behind the brush.

"Spit it out already. How'd it go?"

"He's dead."

Rob yanked on the reins to turn the horse around in a hurry. His eyes scanned the horizon, unable to lock onto any movement that would betray the men he was waiting on. Before he could speak another word, it was Hicks who dared show his face. Moonlight filtered through the pines overhead and cut short by the brush he was hiding in made Hicks almost look normal. His noticeable limp and hand clutching his side gave away a sense of urgency that he no longer had the strength to muster, however.

"What the hell happened to you?"

"Someone was there."

"Where the hell is Hogtie?"

"Back there."

"Cut the shit, Hicks. What's going on?"

"You sent us to a fuckin' death trap, that's what happened!" Hicks exploded right then and there. "We wandered through the damn trees for half the night, found wherever it was you wanted us to break into, and it took five goddamn seconds before Hogtie went and got his head blown off."

"No shit?"

"You think I'm lyin'? Look at me."

"Look fine to me."

"Fuck you!"

"Whoa, whoa," Sam chuckled as he rode up beside Rob.

Just a few seconds later, Cliff made his way up to the other side of Rob. All three remained on their horses, looking down at Hicks, getting more and more furious by the second. There was something about seeing another person's fear overtake them from the back of a horse. The old adage held some truth to it, but rarely did it ever do much good to get down from such a vantage point. From what was seared into Hicks' eyes, Rob knew there was no helping him.

"Hogtie still catching his breath somewhere?" Cliff couldn't help himself.

"How's it feel to denigrate the dead you piece of—"

"Why'd you let him die?" Sam just made matters worse.

"I didn't!"

"Where is he?"

"Why don't you go right back that direction?" Hicks hollered while turning around to point in the general direction behind him. "And go find him your damn self."

"Now calm down," Rob raised his hands.

"No! I ain't goin' back to that shit!"

"Hicks!" Rob finally let his feelings be known. "If you bring someone out here from all that damn hollerin', I promise you I will shoot you dead right where you stand and leave your body for the Colemans, the police, and anyone else who's looking for someone to blame for all this."

"Sir," said Hicks, much more gently this time.

"I swear to high heavens, Hicks. I'll do it."

"Just listen to me."

Silence found its way between the men on the horses and the one looking up at them. It was an unbecoming position for Hicks, and there was little else to do but set the story straight. If this was the position he'd be forced to spill the beans in, then so be it.

Rob watched the man, barely able to stand, take a deep breath. His lungs heaved, and his shoulders dropped. The man looked like he'd been taken out behind the shed and had his shit kicked in for about an hour. It was almost sad to see.

"You pointed out the direction and we followed it until we found a place."

"What kind of place?" Rob already cut them off.

"It was somebody's home. I don't know whose. It just sort of showed up out in the middle of the woods. Didn't see no cars or nothing out front, so Hogtie and me figured no one was home."

"Find out what happens when you walk through a front door in Texas that isn't yours, didn't you?"

"Cliff," Rob cut him off. "Go on, Hicks."

"We didn't, asshole. I cracked open a back window and we both climbed in. No different than we've done a dozen times before. Never have woke anyone or drawn any attention to ourselves. This wasn't a normal home, though. Something was off about it."

"What do you mean?"

"I mean, there wasn't nothing normal inside. There wasn't even a kitchen as far as I could see. All the furniture was covered in plastic, the place reeked of something sour, and I'm not so sure they even had AC. It's like it was abandoned."

"But it wasn't."

"Well, hell no it wasn't. We split up when we got inside. Hogtie went to grab the wallets and all that, like he always does while I try to hit it big. I turn around, not thirty seconds later, and spot a shadow in the darkness before shit went south."

"Who was it?"

"What kind of dumbass question is that? How would I know? The only thing I know is whoever it was knew how to squeeze a damn trigger. Ol' Hogtie didn't even see it coming. One second he was digging around through their shit, and the next, his brains was painted on the wall."

"Apparently, he wasn't that good with a gun. You got out just fine," Sam said, making a point that Rob could only acknowledge with a slight nod, hidden beneath the brim of his cowboy hat.

"I almost didn't. Just got lucky, is all."

"Did you do what I said?" Rob's voice cut through all the fear and paranoia like a warm knife through room-temperature butter. No one else dared respond to his question, but Hicks knew damn well he'd better speak up sooner rather than later.

"Find something worth finding," he repeated the words he was told as he reached into his back pocket and pulled out the black leather notebook he'd stolen. "The people in that house were collectors. I found a room where everything inside looked priceless, and I got my hands on this." He wagged the journal in the air and lifted it higher for his boss to grab.

Rob snatched it out of his hands and jammed it into his jacket pocket, refusing to break eye contact with Hicks for even a second. His horse was every bit as still as he was as they watched Hicks do his best to maintain composure.

"You better hope this proves worthwhile," said Rob.

Chapter 3

You may bear the name of a coward, Robbie, but one day you're gonna learn that a coward's death can sometimes be its own form of justice.

The poetic, depressing words of Rob's father struck him senseless even today, years after his ears were forced to endure such harsh realities about who he was. There was never a moment in his life that wasn't teachable, and more often than not, Rob's father used it to shine a light on the worst parts of who Rob never believed himself to be. He recounted the tale of the coward Robert Ford time and time again, and how it cost the world what he liked to call one of the only pure American legends ever born. Maybe it was a self-fulfilling prophecy, or maybe his father really did know something he didn't. Either way, Rob was still waiting on that day where he'd learn about what a coward's death really meant. Until then, he was forced to kill only time.

In his hands was a wrinkled piece of paper no larger than a sticky note, torn on the edges, stained from years of abuse, and scribbled with nearly illegible writing. Rob's face was empty. He'd stared at the same piece of paper for most of his life. All the disappointment he'd caused, the anger from his inaction, was harbored in that piece of paper. It was his life's work, completed before he'd been given a chance to earn his own way, encapsulated in a single sentence written by a hand more than a hundred and fifty years ago.

By my grandson's grandson, the name Robert Ford will be known all around this miserable world.

Rob's father never faltered in his belief of who this note was referring to. He'd been called the heir to the coward Robert Ford from his birth, carried the name whether he wanted to or not, and was told over and over again what he'd amount to. The words from Rob's father echoed in his head every time he read the torn piece of paper. All the affirmations of his own cowardice, his worst thoughts about himself, had become his whole world.

There was nothing left to do but live up to the name.

So far, he'd done more than enough to fulfill his supposed purpose. He'd abandoned his family and any sense of a home he'd ever known. He'd been a vagabond and a hobo. He'd drifted from one town to the next, stealing enough to get by and never giving so much as a passing glance to those who'd needed him most.

With his self-confidence dwindling lower by the second, Rob allowed himself a moment to look away from the piece of paper in his hands and push away the words of his father swirling in his head. The road passed them by as it always had. They were chasing white lines headed toward the drop off, told to them by none other than the Bossman himself.

The roar of the diesel hauling thousands of pounds of cattle in the twenty-four-foot gooseneck behind them, was a familiar hum from inside the cabin. It lulled Rob in and out of awareness as he reclined back in the passenger seat. He'd made Sam drive him around ever since they had a run-in with a rancher outside of Shelby County about a year ago. They raced down back roads for a couple of hours, avoiding random potshots aimed in their direction before Sam pulled off a turn no one could keep up with. When he watched the rancher roll his old pickup a few times in a pasture behind them, Rob knew right then Sam should be behind the steering wheel.

They were leaving Marion County headed west, about twenty miles down a road Rob had never been down before. He crumpled the piece of paper up in his fist and squeezed so hard his hand turned red as he stared out of the window. It was about fifty degrees outside and raining. Barely recognizable drops of water hit the windshield without making a sound despite driving seventy miles an hour on the two-lane road. A rhythmic dragging sound of the wipers carried on every few seconds. The only lights out on the road were the headlights coming at them and the taillights leaving them behind.

Instead of falling back into the repetitive spiral of his own inadequacies, according to everyone but him, he opted to strike up a nonsense conversation with Sam.

"How much longer?" Rob asked, knowing all too well the directions were on the screen in the truck.

"Says an hour and a half."

"Probably be there by midnight."

The conversation died out as quick as it had started. There weren't any cries of steel guitar playing through the radio or the drone of a jockey who loved the sound of his own voice. There was nothing to distract Rob from his own thoughts. He tried to focus on the frustration building in his gut about having to drive so far with the stolen herd of cattle. It was easy at first, but he couldn't stop his thoughts from drifting, and that usually meant a return to dwelling on the fact that he'd never amount to what he alone knew he was capable of.

A few minutes ticked by in silence before he remembered the one thing Hicks had brought back with him. For a fleeting second, he also remembered the loss of Hogtie, but that wasn't something he would ever be too concerned about. Hogtie was the kind of guy who never said more than a few words, and for good reason. He didn't have anything of value to add. He was the definition of an ass in the saddle.

Rob lifted himself up awkwardly in the passenger seat and reached into his back pocket. The leather journal felt smaller in his hands than he'd realized when he took it from Hicks. It was brittle, yellowed, and frayed, like it had been taken from a museum after a hundred years on display.

As the crooning of a lonesome fiddle was joined by a steel guitar's cry backed by a thumping bass in the door speaker of the diesel truck, Rob stared at the journal without much of an interest. It wasn't until some guy singing interrupted the decent track that Rob felt the need to speak up.

"Can't believe ol' Hogtie got his brains blown out for this damn thing."

Sam didn't take his eyes off the road when he responded. "Seen people die for a lot less. A guy my sister knew had his wheels get stolen right off his car in the parking lot. He hadn't even made it inside the store yet. They shot him dead right then and there when he tried to stop them."

"Jesus."

"Tough to imagine your whole life boiling down to a thousand-dollar set of wheels and tires."

"Probably worth more than this journal. And at least that guy saw it coming."

"Hogtie never really did see much coming, in all fairness."

"He was a big enough target, too."

"True. Don't do much good bein' the broadside of a barn when someone's shooting at you."

Rob finally pinched either side of the leather case of the journal and cracked it open. The dim lighting inside the cab offered just enough light to see what looked like indecipherable scribbles. Despite it being almost impossible to read anything of use, Rob thumbed through the pages and wondered who it could have belonged to.

"It's probably a few months' worth of grocery lists," he commented.

"Maybe it's a list of bank accounts or something useful, you know?"

Sam never did claim to be the brains behind the operation.

Even so, Rob couldn't help but consider the possibility of the journal actually being of use. Maybe it would even lead to a payday for them. He almost let out a chuckle at the pure irony of Hogtie's death, inadvertently pointing the way to something worthwhile.

"Ain't never been that lucky, Sam."

"I don't know about all that. You been on a hot streak lately. How many head does tonight's haul make it? Over a thousand, right?"

"Lost count a while back."

"You know damn well it's better to have a wrong count than no count at all," Sam smarted off. "No matter, you've made plenty of money for the right people. You'll probably be meeting Bossman himself soon if you keep it up."

"As long as he keeps payin', I don't really see a need to know what his face looks like. His money spends just as good as anyone else's."

"You aren't even just a little curious about who it is running this whole thing?"

"I try not to think about it," Rob admitted.

"Well, I'd damn sure like to know who it is signing our checks. Now that we're talkin' about it, how did you get pulled into this whole mess anyway?"

"Got into some trouble years back, didn't have much of a way out," explained Rob.

"What kind of trouble?"

"You wouldn't believe the truth if I told it to you, so I might as well make something up to put a stop to your questions."

"Try me."

"Killed my own father."

Sam couldn't find the words.

"Told you," Rob said.

"No, no, I believe you. Just thinkin' about if I should run while I still can." Sam smirked before he could finish the sentence. "One more question, though."

Rob knew what was coming. It was the same question anyone asked when they found out what he'd done with his life. It could be disguised every which way, but it always boiled down to the same curiosity. Why? He rolled his eyes over to Sam to urge him to get it over with.

"Did he deserve it?"

Rob did his best to hide his surprise. Sam was more adept than he let on at prying information. Unfortunately for him, it was not a subject Rob was eager to dive into, so he gave the only answer he could think of.

"Do any of us?"

Their drive continued through the rain without much discussion until there was no more paved road to be found. Mud slapped against the fender wells as they bounced down the dirt drive winding through the trees. Rob's nerves started to flare as they crept closer. He reached into his canvas jacket pocket, splattered with manure from a job weeks ago, and pulled out a single cigarette and a flick lighter. He cupped his calloused hands over his mouth and pushed his thumb down to strike a flame. After a quick inhale, he brought the cigarette to life and cracked the pickup window all at once.

He held the smoke in his lungs and closed his eyes. The familiar taste of tobacco—and whatever else they packed inside—immediately changed his thoughts. A surge of nicotine helped to steady his breathing. He could feel his vision vibrating from the surge even before he lifted his eyelids. By the time he exhaled, there was only a puff of smoke that escaped his lips before it rushed away through the window at his side.

"Where is this place?" Sam was clearly trying to change the subject.

Rob took another drag on the cigarette and spoke with his chest full of smoke. "Couple miles up."

"Ain't much good happens down roads like this in the middle of the night."

"That's why we ain't the first ones showing up."

Sam took a second to let the words sink in. They hadn't followed anyone there as far as he knew. Rob watched out of the side of his eye as Sam checked his rearview mirrors to confirm his suspicions before finally speaking up. "What does that mean?" Sam said.

"Means I already had that same thought. Dropping off this many pairs in the middle of the night with a bunch of people we've never met just didn't sit right with me. So, I made sure if there was a trap waiting on it, it would be someone else's problem."

Right when he finished talking, Rob's phone began to vibrate inside his jacket pocket. A soft glow soon followed as he pulled it out to see a number neither of the men recognized, trying to call him. With a swipe of this thumb, a man's voice came through the other end.

"About time," Rob told the man.

"You're all good." The man's voice was low, as if he was trying to hide from someone listening in on their conversation.

"You sure about that?" Don't sound so sure."

"I said, you're good."

"Better be." Rob tapped the screen and jammed the phone back into his pocket.

"Should I even ask who that was?"

"Guy who owed me a favor," Rob told Sam with a

smirk. "He wrote more checks than his government paycheck could cash about six months ago. I bailed him out just so I could hold it over his head."

"Remind me not to get on your bad side anytime soon," Sam said.

"Let's just get this over with."

It would only be five awkward minutes before the pickup rolled to a stop. The dirt road that brought them into the middle of nowhere had reached a clearing just large enough to turn around with a trailer. There was an empty circle pen and a short lane made of temporary cattle panels in the distance, but the man they were meant to meet was nowhere to be found.

Sam killed the diesel motor, but left the headlights shining ahead, and for some reason, also the windshield wipers. A faint drizzle of rain almost made the dragging noise worth hearing every few seconds.

"We early?"

"I didn't think four minutes would make much of a difference," Rob said. "I was always taught, if you're on time, you're late."

"Maybe this guy's just on time."

"Maybe."

Rob leaned his seat back and pulled out the black leather journal once again to pass the time. He didn't intend to give much thought to whatever was written inside, but it was about as effective a means available to avoid any further meaningless words with Sam. As good of a hand as he was, there wasn't much going on in that head of his as far as stimulating conversation went.

This time, he opened the journal and flipped through the pages until he landed on the first one. It was pressed against the inside of the cover, stained and discolored, difficult to peel away from the effects of time. Rob was delicate in pulling it back, careful not to rip it. He reached up and flicked on a light inside the cabin and squinted to read the cursive handwriting scribbled inside.

April 8, 1881

> *If not for the rain that went on for days, I never would have been given the opportunity I'd prayed for. Not too long ago, I witnessed my own brother Charles join a cause larger than any one man, even if it was but one man's name known so far and wide. I watched him do what I had long aimed to do myself, and after three days stuck in the mud and muck, it was my turn at last. The James gang wasn't like the others. Not at all. The name wasn't what it once was, yet even then, it was cheered, beloved even, by those who'd been given a chance to know the face of the one who started it all. Newspapers wrote his actions into the pages of history, and stories of his deeds passed from one town to the next with adoration. My brother saw fit to give himself a better life. I wanted more. I wanted for myself what preceded the arrival of the man who made the James gang what it is. Today, I took the first step to a lifelong dream, to a reputation of my own, and most importantly, to fame and renown. The likes of which the world has never seen, nor will likely ever see again.*

Bob.

Rob looked up from the journal only to find the rain was starting to get worse outside. Every drop smacked the windshield louder than the last, before the wipers did their job with a screech that betrayed their age. He stared endlessly into the coming storm found in the headlights, his thoughts swept away by the passage of the journal he'd just read. He debated in his head whether any of it was even real. For a few seconds longer than he'd ever care to admit, he considered the chances that what he was holding was genuine.

The thought passed as quickly as it came.

It was a hapless knock on his passenger window that jerked him back into reality and sent his heart racing. He forgot about the book clutched in his fist as he looked over to find a man's mustachioed face staring at him with a haunting grin stretched from ear to ear. With a muted voice coming from the other side of the door, the man spoke without losing his dreadful smile.

"We're gonna unload right through that gate there, I'll guide ya in," the man hollered. "Name's O'Kelley, by the way. Looks like you're my new boss."

35

Chapter 4

A star pinned onto the chest of a man who knew nothing in life but the relentless pursuit of justice used to mean something.

There was once a time where the badge carried an unmistakable obligation to bend the arc of the world toward the side of righteousness. It was respected, revered, and even feared. There were fewer symbols in the world that could scare a man straight when he found himself spiraling down a path of sin. The star meant safety. It meant sacrifice. It meant impartiality in the face of corruption and immorality.

Through decades of degradation, the badge had become something else. What was once a force of nature for the rule of law had given new meaning to the word crooked. It was no longer about scaring a man straight, it was about using the shadows cast behind the word of law for profit and personal gain. The people knew this. These days, the symbol caused more groans and eye rolling than it did anything else.

It was just another necessary evil in a world overrun by such necessities.

Sheriff Tom T. Turpin, born a hundred miles south of the patch of mud he was standing in, had devoted his life to the star and spent damn near every waking moment chasing after what he knew had to be justice. His straw hat was perched on top of his head like it had been there his entire life. It was worn and dented on the crown, and misshapen in all the wrong spots on the brim. His khaki pearl snap shirt and creased pants may have been given to him as a law enforcement uniform, but the brimstone look in his eye beneath golden aviator sunglasses was something he entered the world with.

"Things just ain't what they used to be anymore," said Tom, as he overlooked a pasture lined with trees in the distance, scanning for anything out of the ordinary. "People ain't the same. They get up to all kinds of nasty shit when they think other people ain't watching them."

He took a step forward and pulled his sunglasses down from his face. The sunlight made his eyes squint as his nostrils flared against the breeze he stood downwind from. Blue skies overhead juxtaposed the dire urgency of the two men who stood just behind.

"How many did y'all say are missing again?"

"At least sixty pairs," a booming voice of a pissed off man came from just behind Tom.

"It's our whole damned herd!"

"We gonna sit here and act like we don't know who it is?" The other one felt the urge to chime in.

"Now, boys," Tom said and turned around to face them both. "John Coleman, I've known you most my whole life. We rode pipelines growin' up almost every weekend for three summers straight. And Sonny, you might be new around here, but I sure ain't. That means if there's some bad people runnin' around who need catching, that's my job. You want to tell me how to do my job?"

"I didn't say—"

"Shut the hell up, Sonny," John cut him off.

"I know where you're cattle are, Mr. Coleman," said Tom. "I know where they're goin' too. Y'all aren't the only ones this is happening to. People are losing head left and right from Cass County down to Angelina. We don't have any reason to believe your cattle are missing or otherwise displaced, either. It's just a matter of gettin' them rounded up and caught."

"I know you don't want us doing your job, sir, but if you know where they are and where they'll be, why can't you just go get them?"

"I wish it were that easy."

John put his hands up above his head and let out a sigh. "I do too, Tom. I do too."

"John!" Another man's frantic voice pierced through the breeze.

"John! John!"

"What the hell do we have here?" Tom asked.

It was his flailing arms and legs that the sheriff saw first. Every couple strides, the approaching man would reach up with his right hand to hold his rolled-up cowboy hat from flying off his head. He weighed only a few more pounds than a skeleton and hid his gaunt face behind an unkempt beard. There was a foul stench in the air at his back. It didn't take long to realize the closer he got, the worse it smelled.

Tom went ahead and pushed the aviators back onto the bridge of his crooked nose and did his best to hide the scowl creeping across his face. He watched as the man sprinted toward them, waving his hands, repeating the same thing over and over again until he was only feet away.

"John! John!"

"God Almighty, Bo. Would you just spit it out already?" John finally told him.

"The pairs are gone! I can't find a single one!"

John and Sonny both pushed their fingers into their eyes. Bo was the hand in charge at this lot. There were few men as loyal, and as stupid, as Bo. Even then, men like him had a certain place only they could hold in an operation like the Coleman Ranch.

Dust flew up into the air behind him, illuminated in the sun's light, blowing away into the air from the breeze still sweeping in. He sucked as much oxygen as his lungs would allow, and did his best to hide his chest from swelling so noticeably.

"I been looking everywhere. I checked down at the bottom, by the creek, and at both the ponds. I'm still tryin' to run the fence lines. I'll find them, though, sir," Bo explained.

"I sure wish your parents weren't dead, Bo. Because I'd like to slap the shit out of both of them for dropping you on your head one too many damned times," said John.

Before Tom had a chance to intervene, he felt a rumble on his hip before static interrupted them all. His radio was going off. There was a woman beckoning him by name on the other end, and he knew there'd be hell to pay if he didn't see what was going on. Denise was an old soul. Most would credit her as the backbone of the entire dispatch department. Tom had come to know her as something else, though. He was lucky enough to have seen a different side of her back when she was first given her job and helped teach her the ins and outs of what they didn't teach in school. Because of this, he was able to be among the few who called her a friend.

Denise's voice finally cleared up through the static. She was calling out codes, repeating them until Tom gave her the go-ahead. He was hard of hearing, and Denise knew as much. Her repetition was her way of being kind.

"I'm here, I'm here," he spoke into a corded microphone he had to yank off a belt loop on his hip. "What's goin' on?"

"We got an anonymous tip in," she said.

Tom turned to walk away from the men still bickering about the stolen cattle and walked away. There wasn't much in the way of privacy nearby, but from the tension in the argument happening without him, the men had no interest in what he was talking about.

"Hit me."

"A line of trailers were headed out of town in the middle of the night. Some old woman called in a complaint about them doing sixty in a fifty-five, described more than half a dozen matching trucks and cattle trailers speeding by her and almost scaring her off the road. Seems like something you'd want to know about."

"Did you run the plates on the woman who called it in?"

"Oklahoma, sir."

"I'm telling you, every time."

"I'm starting to think you're right," Denise said, with a hint of humor creeping into her tone.

"That was definitely our boys, though." Tom straightened himself up. "Find out which way they were headed, will you?"

"Already did."

"Have I told you that you deserve a raise?"

"Traveling west on forty-nine, leaving the county."

"No surprise there."

"I'm gonna kick your ass for sayin' that!" Sonny's voice cried out suddenly.

"Ah, shit," said Tom.

"You better run, you son of a bitch!"

"Denise, have I ever told you I'd like to join the dispatch team one day?"

"Go get 'em, Tom," she responded before the radio speaker on Tom's hip turned once

again to white noise.

By the time Tom had turned back around to see what all the hollering was about, Sonny had already put Bo right on his back in the mud. His fists were stained red, and he was blurting out one obscenity after another. It was an understandable fight, all things considered. From the few seconds that Tom had listened to Bo speak his mind, he knew there wasn't too much going on up there.

Even then, it was times like this where the star meant a different kind of obligation. He couldn't just let Sonny beat the daylights out of Bo just because he earned it. He was meant to put a stop to such violence. That didn't mean he had to be in much of a hurry, though.

He walked slow and steady over to Sonny and put his hand on the attacker's shoulder. Sonny's fists slowed to a halt. For some reason, the only thing he couldn't stop by showing his face was Bo's rambling, even after so many blows to the face. If anything, the fight had made it worse.

"I'm sorry boss, I'm sorry boss," he kept saying as blood began to stream down his cheek.

Sonny didn't care much to look around him as he wailed on poor Bo's face, turning it all kinds of black and blue. If he had, he would've seen Tom standing over his shoulder, staring down at him. It wasn't until he felt the calloused backside of the sheriff's hand swiping across his head that he finally stopped swinging at Bo.

"What the hell was that for?"

"Stand up, Sonny. You too, Bo," said Tom. "Now, I want all three of you to stay right here while I go talk to a couple more people who got roped into all this mess."

"There were witnesses?" John asked. "Did they say where they went? Why're you standing around here when we don't know a damn thing? Go figure out what they know!"

Tom pulled his aviators down the bridge of his nose and glared at John. There was an anger building up in his belly. It was the kind of anger his doctor had said would put him in the hospital one day. He was already taking too many pills every day to keep trudging along. This kind of outburst was exactly what he was told to shrug off.

Without so much as a faulty exhale, Tom turned to walk back to his F150 pickup parked in a dirt easement road running alongside a patch of tree, brush, and briar. The truck had been with him for more than two hundred thousand miles, and it hadn't failed him once in all that time. Today, it would be the only thing keeping him from making John's face look a lot like Bo's did at the moment.

The familiar dinging sound in his ears helped to distract him as he slid into the worn driver's seat. A trace of cigar smoke lingered inside the pickup, a welcome change of pace from the pollen polluting the air. By the time he had brought the old V6 motor to life and thrown the shifter down into reverse, his phone was demanding his attention from inside his pocket. He squeezed it to silence the ringer and went on about his business.

His drive to the address he had scribbled down on a yellow sticky note turned out to be a short one. It was just a few minutes down the road before he found himself turning down a winding driveway through a picturesque view of bald cypress and pine trees towering above him. For a few seconds, he allowed himself the opportunity to soak in the surroundings. They may have been just outside the border of the nearby Caddo Lake State Park, but it was every bit as beautiful as the cordoned-off areas.

It was the familiar dull hum of white noise coming from his radio that broke him out of his momentary peace. Once again, it was Denise on the other end.

"I see you're headed to the house that called in," she said. "You are looking for two adults, one Native woman and one White male. It was the woman who fired the shot, in case you were wondering."

"You read my mind, Denise, as always."

"How's the victim?"

"Deceased."

"You ever wonder why these people are willing to die over a couple of wallets and some jewelry?"

"Not unless it's our job to figure it out. In this case, it doesn't really matter why people do the things they do."

"I guess you're right. Nothing's gonna change the fact that man's dead."

"With any luck, we can prevent the next one."

"You're too good for this world, Denise."

White noise returned to the radio. It took a moment before Tom reached down to click it off. The silence that fell over the cabin of the pickup was immeasurably worse in his opinion. This was broken up immediately by the ringing of his cell phone once again. Just like clockwork, he reached down and squeezed the phone once again to return the pickup to silence. Road noise was better than that cursed cell phone.

This time, it rang again, though.

"Son of a…" Tom trailed off as he jammed his hand down into his pocket to retrieve the phone.

After a quick glance down to see the number lighting up the screen, he mindlessly tapped a red X to send the call right to voicemail. The number wasn't saved in his phone under any contact, but he knew there was only one person calling from a 713 area code. And it wasn't time to talk to that person just yet.

His eyes darted back to the winding driveway just in time to see his path blocked by a 3500 dually truck parked sideways. His boot hit the brake pedal, and dust flew up behind him in rooster tails that faded into clouds threatening to envelope both vehicles. His F150 slid to a stop and sent Tom bouncing forward in his seat, slamming into the steering wheel. He threw the shifter into park, adjusted his aviators on his face, and threw the door open, cussing and snorting loud enough for anyone nearby to hear.

"I swear on my momma's decaying grave in the dirt I'll put you six foot under the mother—"

He stopped talking when the window began to roll down. He'd know that graying beard stretching down and soulless black eyes anywhere. His name was Dalton D. Woodson and he was one seriously pissed off man. The phone calls Tom had been ignoring sure didn't help his mood, but there was something else Tom was meant to answer for.

"Tom," the man's voice was deep and raspy. He was the kind of man who wore a black felt cowboy hat no matter the time of year. Customary seasonal use of a straw hat just didn't sit right with him for some reason. Beneath the brim of his cowboy hat were eyes that could look right through Tom. After only saying his name, Dalton was already putting his glare to use. "Why am I here right now?"

"Well," Tom began to stutter. "I know what you're about to say—"

"You do? You know what I'm thinking?"

The door flew open, catching Tom off guard and smacking him right in the chest. Before he knew what was happening, the sheriff was on his ass in the dirt, and Dalton was standing over the top of him.

Dalton was every bit of three hundred pounds. His starched denim jeans and stitched leather boots matched with a denim pearl snap featuring an unmistakable logo embroidered onto the chest. Tom knew what it was. The backward lazy letter D paired with the letter W was a brand for one of the largest cow-calf operations in the state of Texas. He was more than a ten-thousand-acre landowner and sixth-generation cattleman. He was a magnate. He was a baron of industry. Most importantly, though, he was not to be trifled with.

Thomas looked up at the hulking man hunched over, staring down at him with black holes for eyes. He did his best to start explaining. At first, it was only frantic breaths that escaped his lips, but he was able to find a few words before his situation worsened.

"They're already on their way," said Tom. "I'm not doing anything but tying up loose ends here. I promise."

To the sheriff's surprise, there were no cruel words or threats that met his reasoning. Instead, a hand twice the size of his with stubby fingernails and freckles reached out toward him. He grabbed it and lifted himself up out of the earth.

Dalton smiled big at Tom and used his oversized hands to brush the dirt off the sheriff's shoulders. When he ended his kind gesture with a friendly pat on the shoulder, Tom knew he'd better not say whatever he was thinking. At this point, it would be best to just wait for Dalton to do what he had to do.

"I got a lot of people comin' in on Friday," Dalton said with a frozen smirk. "It's going to be a good day. I just want you to know that before you go off to play cops and robbers with all those folks."

"I understand, Mr. Woodson."

"That means there's gonna be a lot of money comin' this way," the burly man continued. "It means there's also gonna be a lot of money comin' your way."

"You know how much I appreciate what you do."

Another pat on his shoulder came from Dalton. "You remember all those good things we're gonna do for the people, right?"

The sheriff knew what was happening, and he knew any hesitation could mean certain disaster if taken the wrong way. "Yes, sir," he answered as quickly as he could.

"Just wanted to make sure you didn't forget," said Dalton. "That's all."

Chapter 5

It was the moonlight of yet another night, filtering through the loblolly pines reaching into the sky, doing its best to illuminate the way to another ransom let out to roam the pastures.

Rob had never been the trusting type. He was instinctively cautious. If anyone ever did slip up and get cross with him, he was as obstinate as they come. Not much could change his mind once he'd made it up. To him, separation was something he could control. This had served him well through the years as he always sought to distance himself from anyone, or anything that might cause him harm.

A rhythmic, gentle rise and fall from riding in the saddle got him thinking. The men he worked with knew a lot about him, especially about what he got up to in the middle of the night. If there was a time to start thinking about moving on, he was more than likely long past giving it the time of day. His boots resting on the saddle stirrups and his hands gripping the leather reins always had proven to be his best time to think. For a few fleeting seconds, he pondered the process and its most likely outcome, all the way to his own disappearance from a life of thievery and crime. What a world it could be. It wasn't even close to impossible, either. He could just tug the reins in one direction and keep riding.

But he never did.

He always doubled down on the worst things in life, like he had no other choice but to disappoint. It wasn't some misguided hope for eventual success. It was simply what was in front of him. Rustling was just what he happened to get roped into. He'd be lying to himself if he said he wasn't terrified by the possibility of throwing his whole life into turmoil.

His thoughts remained on the conflict of motives that burned in his belly, telling him to run for the hills one second, and remain to do what is easiest the second. It was enough of a headache to cause Rob to pinch another cigarette and pluck it into his lips. The first drag cast aside any thoughts of fleeing. The second reassured him there was no other way but forward in the life he led.

After another overly long exhale of blue smoke, he plucked the cigarette into his lips and flicked the lighter once again, this time holding the flame steady. In his other hand, he grasped the same black leather journal from before. It was wedged between his fingers alongside the reins, loosely keeping his horse headed in the right direction. Any distraction from his own spiraling was more than welcome. For a reason he couldn't explain, his thoughts drifted back to what was written inside.

May 13, 1881

It was lonesome on the run. They all warned me it would be, but I don't mind it. We rode in on some family's patch of dirt the night before and let ourselves in. Never done that before. The look on their faces are burned into me. They told us no, but he didn't pay much attention. The beds were warm, so was the food. There was a rifle hung above the door. It was a promise for people just like me. That's why I sleep with my Colt in my fingers. You never know when you will be called upon to use it. Today turned out to be my day. I never gave much thought to how much gunpowder stinks before I pulled the trigger. It's all I can think about now. It wasn't his blood or the look in his eye that I keep coming back to. I smell gunpowder with every breath, and I am starting to wonder if it's my own just punishment, bestowed by a hand above for what I'd done. No matter, because his ten head of cattle were ours now. They were down to their bones. Probably all that family had left to survive on. At least they won't have to worry about that. Rustling had never taken a liking to me in the past, but boss says he has it all figured out. He always does. Still, I wonder if such death was warranted. They never talked about this in the dime novels I carry around in my saddlebags. I wonder if I get a higher cut being that I pulled the trigger?

Bob.

"Is it much further up?" Cliff's voice came from behind Rob, drifting in like a wakeup call in the middle of a dream he didn't even realize he'd fallen into.

"I wouldn't sink too deep in that saddle," Sam answered for Rob.

"We should've made the new guy pack in some whiskey."

"You know damn well that wouldn't make tonight any easier."

"This ain't my first time bein' the new guy," O'Kelley chimed in from the rear of the line of horses. "What if I was to say I packed enough whiskey to kill this here horse y'all gave me?"

"No kiddin'?" Cliff turned in his saddle to make eye contact with O'Kelley. Instead of a witty comment or some long-winded explanation, he was met with a bottle tossed in his direction.

"Think we got ourselves a winner," said Sam.

Rob refused to dignify what was happening with a response. He wasn't against drowning at the bottom of a bottle by any means, but not while he was working. There was too much that could go wrong. "Save it for when we're done, Cliff," he finally said, jamming the worn journal back into his jacket pocket. "This is gonna play out just like we went over back at the trailers. O'Kelly, you ain't done this with us before, so you hang back and feel it out. No cuttin'. No playin' cowboy. Just let Sam and Cliff do the hard work. You and I can push. No moseying around neither, we're in and out, just like that."

"Where did all those trailers come from, anyways?" Sam couldn't help but ask.

"Looks like more than double what we had last time."

"Whoever is signing our checks should start thinking about buying some eighteen-wheelers or something," Sam continued. "Not sure if there are enough goosenecks in the county to do whatever Bossman is really after."

"That kind of thinking is above all of our paygrades, Sam," said Rob. "Best thing we can do is put our heads down and get it done. Even if you knew the answers to all those questions, it wouldn't change the fact you still gotta do whatever Bossman says. Save yourself the trouble, don't worry about nothing you can't control."

"I know you don't want to hear this, Rob," Sam started. "But we always got control of our own lives. Even if we don't wanna admit it."

"I didn't know you were a damn therapist."

"I don't know about all that. But now that you brought it up, do y'all ever think about what it'd be like to actually talk to one of those quacks?"

Cliff was the first one to take Sam's bait. "Every time I'm forced to be around you for more than an hour."

"No, really," Sam started in. "All these people do is sit around and talk about what they feel like, but they don't never go out and do anything about it. Always seemed like a surefire way to get the blues to me."

"You ever actually hear yourself talk, dipshit?"

"The hell does that mean? I'm bein' serious here."

"They *are* doin' something about it. They're at the damn therapist for Chrissake."

"That ain't what I'm talking about. I'm talking about swiping a wallet if you don't have any money, or taking all those free samples at the grocery store when you're starving."

"You know, Sam, if there was anybody in this outfit who needed to go see a therapist, it'd be you."

"Let me put it this way," Sam said. "Let's say a guy walks up and punches you right square in the chin, for no good reason. Are you gonna throw a haymaker at his stupid face or go home and tell some guy in a fancy suit how much it hurt?"

"Only thing you're gonna do by goin' off and beating some guy's face in is sit your ass in jail right next to him. Then what're you gonna do?"

"At least I'll feel better about it."

"Maybe you could've felt better about it without gettin' put in jail with the asshole who punched you in the first place?"

"How you figure?"

"A fuckin' therapist!" Cliff was about to lose it.

"All right, both of you, cut the shit," Rob finally had to interject.

The silence that fell over the group of men riding around on horseback in a pasture that wasn't theirs was both awkward and entirely welcome. It was a moment of peace rarely ever had in their line of work. As annoyed as Rob could get with the men he rode with, he knew if anything went south, they were just the kind of men he needed. Not to save his ass or anything like that, but to take the fall when he couldn't. These men were the salt of the earth, but they were also run-of-the-mill. They could be replaced, no better or worse than he could.

Just as the thought crossed his mind, he turned to look at their newest member, riding close by to him and doing a dang good job at keeping his mouth shut. New guys were usually more adept to not drawing too much attention to themselves on the first day of the job, but this man was quieter than Hicks, who'd been lost in a spiral of self-deprecation ever since Hogtie's untimely end. It was odd. Rob considered striking up a halfhearted conversation to feel him out, but thought better of it and decided to keep his mouth shut as well.

For the first time in more than a week, they were riding around on land that didn't belong to the

Coleman Ranch. They had at long last stepped foot into a three hundred-acre plot of land that belonged to a man named Adam Barnes. He wasn't rich. He didn't own some ranching empire. He didn't even have anything in the way of a family. He was just Adam, and he was a complete dick.

You didn't have to be from anywhere in East Texas to know Adam was about as unlikable as a splinter wedged under a fingernail when it was freezing outside. It just so happened that he just decided to get into the cattle business, too. With the market as high as it was, he probably thought it was an easy few bucks. Rob and his outfit had been told the hundred and fifty head were malnourished, and because of it, easily recognizable. Adam was the kind of guy who thought it was unnecessary to do anything like feed or doctor so much as a single calf. In the back of his head, Rob fought back the urge to go so far as to think they would be doing the cattle a favor.

"Look what we got here," Sam said, finally breaking the silence after a half hour.

There were slight twinkles in the night, what looked like hundreds of reflections staring like demons coming out of pits swallowed in darkness. Pairs of eyes dotted the pasture in front of Rob and his cowboys, trailing close behind. They were everywhere. Cicadas hummed a chorus of screeching that lulled the cattle into chewing their cud and laying down for the night. Stars stretched out overhead, refusing to be dimmed by the moon's light.

It was a sight to behold, but Rob could only see dollar signs. Thousands of dollars floated above the head of every cow, magnified by the pairs among them, and categorized by weight. They were black-hided, which pretty much checked all the boxes needed to be certified, for whatever good that meant. It didn't matter that their hip bones jutted out on either side and they barely had enough fat to stay warm at night, they'd fill the order all the same.

"Let's get to work, boys," said Rob.

Like clockwork, the rustlers fanned out across the pasture in silence. Their coordination was unspoken and intuitive as they moved through the herd. Their aim was to position themselves across the pasture and push the herd back in the direction they came. It was a crap shoot with cattle like this, though, impossible to tell which were docile and which were crazed. The only way they could know for certain was to get started.

It took only minutes before the first cries rang out and the work at hand truly kicked off. A whirlwind of hooves, bellering, and rope tore through the woods. Dirt replaced any breath of air available, and within minutes, Rob and his cowboys had bandannas pulled over their faces, showing only squinted glares beneath their cowboys hats as they pushed the herd onward.

"Go on!"

"Git!"

The familiar whooping and hollering silenced the cicadas and sent grasshoppers flying from the path of the cattle. They moved by starlight alone, corralling loose calves and preventing strays from separating. It took minutes before Rob was able to reach a count of one hundred fifty. Exactly what he'd been told to round up.

It was easy going, until it wasn't.

When you work with cattle long enough, you learn how they think, how they react, and you learn how to follow their lead every bit as much as they follow yours. It was a telltale sign that told Rob they were in trouble before they knew what was happening, and it all started with a single cow lifting her head up into the sky and slamming on the brakes. Her hooves dug into the mud, and she planted herself still. The pile up that followed looked like a black mass of shadow enveloping itself as the cattle toppled forward over the only one among them too stubborn to go with the flow.

It was enough to send Rob's chest fluttering, but the gunshot that blasted out through the trees just on the other side of the hill was enough to do him in right then and there. A muzzle blast spewed into the air like a flare signaling their doom. What was once a well-oiled operation pushing a herd of one hundred fifty cattle to a line of trailers waiting at the other end of the property soon turned to hellish chaos.

"Shit!" Hicks was the first to cry out in fear.

"Split up! Sam, you go east! Cliff, you're west! Get the strays rounded up and get every single one right back here," said Rob. Barking orders wasn't something he was unfamiliar with, but doing it while getting shot at would always be a challenge. It wasn't something anyone could ever just get used to.

"Hicks!" Rob continued to yell. "You go find whoever the hell that was!"

The words that came in response fell upon Rob's ears like a ton of bricks.

"You go do it!" Hicks hollered back. "I ain't goin' back to that house. You ain't gonna catch me goin' in there for one goddamned second. Not after what I seen."

"The hell are you talkin' about, Hicks?"

"You can't make me!"

It was pitch black, and they were surrounded by a stampede of freaked-out cattle, confused about the safest direction to run. Even so, Rob knew just where to turn his attention and stare a hole right through Hicks.

"Do it, or I shoot you right here and now," Rob hollered. "You won't ever have to worry about anything ever again."

"Son of —"

The one who fired the shot still hadn't come out from beyond the horizon in the distance. Rob became consumed by the mystery of who was upending their work. He watched Sam and Cliff do what they did best, likely the only two real cowboys among them, and gave up any hope of Hicks or the new guy making themselves useful. He grinded his teeth together one last time and heeled his horse forward.

His mind raced as tunnel vision closed in around him. The bouncing of his saddle became his only focus. His outfit would have assumed Rob was running in the direction of the gunshot, that he was doing what any good leader should, and solving the problem by himself. Instead, he'd turned his horse and beckoned the beast to sprint as far away in the opposite direction as possible.

He rushed over the hill, never looking back, fully committed to leaving his entire life behind him. It was a decision he hadn't given much thought to. It was also a decision made in less than a split second. He was never beholden to his cowboys, or the boss who paid him just enough to get trapped into a life on the run. Why couldn't he just leave? Why couldn't he run? The plan falling apart was just enough of a reason to chase a different kind of life. All he had to do was get away.

The next thirty seconds happened as a blur. He reached the top of the hill and almost fell off his horse as he saw a man holding a rifle already facing him down. The gun was aimed at his chest, and the man's finger was ready to squeeze the trigger. Rob's horse raced toward the man Rob could only assume was Adam, regardless of the danger he posed. Out of sight of any of the cowboys still dealing with the herd, Rob felt his fingers on the handle of his six-shooter he hoped to never use.

It was the last thing he felt before a burst of flame reached forth and a cry from the end of a barrel rang out into the night.

Chapter 6

"I wasn't too sure what was goin' on at first, but you damn sure did!"

"Looked like you was runnin' away."

"Hell, I knew all along what you was up to. I knew you were one step ahead of us the whole time."

Sam, Cliff, and even Hicks had found their way back to Rob's side. He didn't pay them any attention. He was standing over a body. Unflinching, careless death rode with him, and he had only just now known of its presence. It was a cold hand, and Rob could feel its weight on his shoulder. He was only trying to run. It was a fleeting feeling that had already passed, leaving him reeling from his own worst judgment. Lifeless eyes staring up were mirrored in his own. He couldn't look away, and for a reason even he struggled to believe—he didn't want to.

"That must've been ol' Adam," said Cliff. "This is something he would do. Always was a dumbass."

Sam kneeled down beside the body of Adam Barnes. Blood was pooling beside his shoulders, and any sounds of life had long faded away. Without thinking about DNA evidence, fingerprints, or investigations into the loss of a life, Sam pushed his fingers on Adam's neck and then leaned his head down to listen to his chest. After closing his eyes for a few emotional seconds of silence, he finally spoke up and said, "Yeah, he's dead."

"You really are a dumbass," Cliff said. "You don't see the bloody, gaping hole in the side of his face? Of course he's dead."

"We still want to be sure. You never know."

"Of what?" Hicks chimed in, somehow fully aware of what was going on and what Sam had just suggested.

"I'm not fallin' for your shit this time, Sam," said Cliff. "We don't have much time before this turns a heck of a lot worse. Rob, any ideas?"

"Bring him."

All of the men stared ahead in silence as they considered everything that was required to pull off what Rob had just requested. It was twisted to even consider, unthinkable to most with even a basic understanding of morality. Adam may have been a well-known asshole, especially considering what he did when no one was looking in his direction, but there were some men who did more than turn from God's eye in their own wallowing. These men would always deserve the chair, or worse. Adam was not among those men. He didn't deserve the fate that had befallen him, delivered by lead and gunpowder.

Rob climbed back on his horse, holstered the pistol still locked in his grip, and hardened his glare at the cowboys who stood below him. They were huddled around Adam's body, mostly confused or bewildered, but ready to do what they were told. Despite the shiver that went down each of their spines and the metallic tingle hitting their noses from the blood loss soaking into the dirt, they never faltered in working together, as a team.

When Rob refused to clarify what he meant, the men agreed they were being told to literally bring him along as they finished the job they'd set out to do. This was hammered out through a conflict-fueled conversation between the cowboys. As Rob rode away at a slow pace and in the direction of the stolen herd up ahead, the men he left behind to do the dirty work had a decision to make.

Who was going to carry the body?

The old saying about skinning a cat was perfectly applicable here. However, to the men standing around Adam's still-warm body, there was only one mutually respected method that could be used in such a dilemma. It was a non-bias, universally understood agreement, where each of the men would be unequivocally bound to the results.

Three fists rose into the air, and they came down a couple of times methodically before each man made their choice. Only one was an oddball sign coming down during the impromptu game. Two hands came back as scissors, and one unfortunately came down as a piece of paper.

"That's horse shit!" Hicks said. "I always pick paper. Wins every time, I swear!"

"Didn't this time."

"Don't get blood everywhere either."

"Y'all gotta at least help me get him up there," said Hicks. "Can't expect me to do it all by myself."

Sam and Cliff looked at each other and squinted.

They didn't even have to say anything. Two more fists rose into the air with reinvigorated purpose. This time, one first came right back down, and one opened into paper. The smirk that formed on Sam's face as he rode off was borderline evil.

The group rode along beneath the shining stars above, stubbornly permanent when nothing else dared to be, lighting their way back to their original destination. A fleet of gooseneck trailers never held as much promise as the ones waiting on their arrival. They were the only real ticket to putting this entire night behind them. It was supposed to be just another job, not a forsaken nightmare.

Rob led the push back. His mind stayed fixed on the escape that was almost his. Every one of the cowboys stuck doing what they were doing dreamed of a life they couldn't have. Few were able to ever make it happen. Rob was close, but the line of business he was in had a unique way of roping you back, no matter how hard you tried to run.

He was once again drifting in and out of awareness, lulled deeper into his thoughts by the trampling of the cattle and the rattling of his outfit, complaining as usual. It all turned to static. He could feel his fingertips buzzing, yearning to yank the reins and make another run for it. He knew deep down that wasn't an option now, though. There was a dead man riding alongside them, and if there was one thing Rob had learned in the hardest of ways—it was that death always came at a cost.

Their ride would continue on without end, into an eternity where Rob was a cold-blooded killer for the second time in his life. A wish of escaping clung to the furthest reaches of his mind while he suppressed the urge to dwell on what had just happened. The feeling of the pistol in his grip, how it felt just a little bit lighter after the bullet was fired, and how the stench of gunpowder mixed with blood would never again leave his nostrils all confirmed what had just happened, no matter if he denied it. Adam's last face he'd ever make was one he'd see in his sleep. The time it took them to follow their tracks back was more than he could stand as such thoughts swirled on and on.

The stars were blocked by the trees that had swallowed them up. A cool breeze turned to stifling humidity in a matter of hours. Songs of cicadas and grasshoppers and cattle on the move were silenced in a deafening darkness broken only by hooves pounding the dirt. It was enough to make Rob wish he were mad. He pretended he was unchanged by the night he only barely survived, he even allowed an occasional emotionless chuckle to match the others when Hicks complained about the unfairness of his situation in great detail. Still, their ride couldn't end soon enough, and it seemed keen on dragging out for the remainder of Rob's lifetime.

Finally, a familiar echo came through the woods. It was a roar of a fleet ready to do the work of a hundred cowboys across a hundred miles. They arrived at the line of trailers waiting with diesels running and men standing around waiting to get to work. The cattle were all too eager to leave their misfortunes behind, a sentiment that matched the men pushing them onto the trailer. Rob never really did come back into thinking clearly, but he did allow himself a simple distraction while he helped to sort what few pairs were among the herd. His voice cracked at first, but he soon found the solace he so desperately sought.

I've never seen a night so long,
And time goes crawling by.
The moon just went behind the clouds,
To hide its face and cry.

"I didn't realize we got a concert at the end of every job," O'Kelley said, feeling a little too comfortable for his first night. "Who sang that one again?"

"It was—"

"That's right. You should let me sing it."

The new guy's attempt to make light of the situation fell flat and on deaf ears. Sam and Cliff were dealing with a particularly unruly set of calves, and Hicks still had his own problem to deal with on the back of his horse. Rob was the only one with enough sense to pay attention, and he couldn't help himself but to stare endlessly through O'Kelley as he laughed at his own misplaced joke. There was something about his face that Rob found impossibly infuriating. For a few passing seconds, he thought maybe if the first person he had gunned down had a face like that, he wouldn't feel so bad. Instead, he let it all pass and ignored the rookie, choosing to get back to work.

It wasn't a question of what he had to do next. It was a matter of whether or not he even wanted to. There were certainly more ways to escape the life he was in, and they didn't all involve his own freedom. Ultimately, even he knew there wasn't really any question about what he would do. He had to save himself.

After the cattle were loaded, the trailers locked up, and the diesel pickups were pulling away, it was finally time to make the phone call he never wanted to make. It was described as an emergency line, and if Hicks' antics were any indication, the situation he'd put them all in damn sure qualified as an emergency.

He stared into the abyss beyond the trees and imagined anything his mind would allow, anything other than the call ringing on the other line in his ear. It rang three times before it clicked, and a faint trace of a man breathing came through. Rob hesitated to say anything, but he knew there was no choice now.

"Encajuelado," Rob said.

The breathing paused just for a moment, then the voice on the other end came through. "The cost is steep, and you haven't finished paying for the last one. You sure, Rob?"

"I was told all I had to say to get rid of a body again was—"

The phone beeped twice in Rob's ear as the call was cut short.

Chapter 7

The DW Ranch was an empire all its own.

Ten thousand acres stretching out in every direction represented the kind of wealth that couldn't be obtained in today's world. If you wanted to call yourself an owner of even a tenth of what the DW Ranch stood upon, you would need to inherit every acre. Staked out in the 1800s by a man with enough foresight to set up a livelihood for his grandchildren's grandchildren, the DW Ranch was as much of a tourist destination as it was a pioneer in cattle genetics and market opportunities.

Just pulling down the driveway was nothing short of a time machine to a lifestyle long thought to be dead and gone. It was several miles and wound through pasture after pasture, lined with immaculate oaks that had reached maturity decades ago. The sun rising in the east cast a glorious glow over the fields, fertilized and lush, grazed only by the cattle hand-selected to represent the best of what the ranch had to offer for those who entered through the gates.

It was picturesque, unchanged for years and years. The grass was fertilized and the trees were trimmed, the hay rings were manicured, and cattle were pristine; even the paved driveway had not so much as a single crack running through it.

Perfection was the word that came to Sheriff Tom Turpin's mind, but he knew better. He knew what crawled around in the underbelly of empires.

He stayed on the winding driveway for what seemed like twenty minutes. It took him around a series of barns with silos towering out front, between a small neighborhood of brick homes, the sheriff could only assume were for the hands who worked the land, and finally, beneath a twelve-foot-wide banner stretched over the pavement that read *DW Ranch's 175th Community Futurity Auction & Benefit*. The banner seemed to be 175 years old itself. It was yellowed and cracked, but impossible to miss.

Just as the sheriff drove his old F150 beneath the banner, his phone began to vibrate from inside the cup holder in the center console. He glanced down at the screen and considered not even picking it up. It was a world he longed for. One day, he'd take that phone out to his family's old acre and a half pond and toss it as hard as he could. Watching the cursed device sink to the bottom would be the only retirement celebration he'd ever need. For now, unfortunately, he had no choice but to do the dreaded swipe and push it to his ear.

"Calling you here instead of your radio," Denise's warm voice came through. "I have something for you."

"I sure hope it's my retirement papers."

"One of those days, huh?"

"I'm just bein' a grouch. What you got?"

"I've been looking into public records of the ranch you told me about. Property taxes, real estate purchases, licensing, and even litigation filings."

"What kind of litigation?"

"The kind that would make me want to call you on your personal cell phone."

"That's what I thought. I need you to send me everything you found right now, then get back to it. If one day of digging is already producing results, imagine what a few weeks will turn up."

"Already done, but I have to warn you, whatever it is you think you are uncovering, it might be more than you can handle. You aren't in your indestructible twenties anymore."

"How bad can it be? We've handled just about every type of criminal that walks one way or another."

Denise paused for just a moment. The hesitation sent Tom's thoughts into a frenzy, but her tone confirmed his worst suspicions when she decided to speak up again.

"Just be careful, that's all I'm saying."

"I always am, Denise. Thanks."

His thumb was twice the size of the red button on the screen he had to hit to end the conversation, but it was always his favorite part of any call. He tossed the phone back into the cupholder with a *thunk* that rattled the change inside his center console. His mind was already on the potential dirt he'd have in his back pocket if things went his way. The possibilities almost made him giddy. There was no time to lose himself in hypotheticals, though.

His truck rolled to a stop on the outside of a makeshift parking lot out in the middle of a pasture. A dirt road connected the parking lot to a massive steel warehouse that looked more like a coal factory than an event center. Despite its appearance, anyone who was anyone in a few hundred-mile radius had made their way to the ranch to join the annual fundraiser. It was a sea of cowboy-hat-donning men and their wives covered in gaudy jewelry, all walking in a line as wide as the road itself.

It was as much of a fashion show as it was a bene-fit. Sheriff Turpin was underdressed, as usual, but that never stopped him from crashing a party he wasn't invited to. He tossed his trusty straw cowboy hat on top of his head, knowing all too well it would be the only one that looked like it was worn in the last year, and made his way into the trail of people. No one cared enough about his badge to pay much attention. That wasn't what bothered him, though. As it was every year, the thorn in his side about the annual DW Ranch Community Futurity Auction & Benefit was the fact that there wasn't a single member of the community in attendance.

There were no familiar faces. There were no warm smiles and hugs of friends coming together again. There weren't even any local organizations trying to raise a few bucks of their own off the crowd. It was always new faces, and they always brought more money every year, no matter what. This was something Tom knew the owner of the DW Ranch prided himself on. Dalton D. Woodson was a self-made man, and these were the people who'd paid for his empire. It really was as simple as that.

Tom pretended not to know what the men did for a living as he brushed past them. Their fancy brand boots with jewelry that likely cost more than he made in a year belied a type of income that he struggled to even imagine. He had long pushed aside his curiosity about what attracted them to the ranch, however, as those suspicions were put to rest the minute he met Mr. Woodson.

Most empires these days were built through inheritance. It typically took generations of discipline and hard work to create an operation that could sustain itself and support so many members of the family who built it decade after decade. There were ranches in America built on the frontier of the Wild West that still stood the test of time today. Men who stood on the shoulders of their ancestors wielded rope and machine-like weapons of war to cultivate a lifestyle that could withstand the pressures of the always-changing world around them.

The DW Ranch was not among these empires.

The DW Ranch was built in a single lifetime. It was built by the hands of Dalton alone, through means most never really came to understand. Thousands of acres were gobbled up in only a few years in a new age market where most deemed it a miracle to afford even ten acres. The most frightening part was that it seemed he had no intention of slowing down anytime soon.

Most people just assumed he moved to Texas from California, or New York, but Tom knew what kind of man Dalton was. He didn't come from money, but he damn sure knew how to make it come to him—by any means necessary.

When he walked between the thirty-foot barn doors that framed the entry into the convention center, Tom remembered the year 1977 for the first time in decades. Elvis had just died, and the radios talked about it nonstop every hour of the day. Liquor was his water, just as it was everyone else's. There was gambling and bare-knuckle fighting, crowds of men surrounding every woman, wallets deeper than ever, thanks to unsavory means, and music loud enough to vibrate your nervous system, making you feel every note literally in your bones. This was the kind of place Tom should have never been, but it was also the kind of place that he could recognize in an instant for the rest of his life.

There were two shirtless men pummeling each other's faces with bloody fists in a makeshift boxing ring where dozens of men stood around laughing with wads of cash in their own fists. Scantily dressed women strutted by with drinks balanced in one hand and blowing kisses at men who shouldn't have even been looking in their direction. Against the back wall sat a stage where a man with headphones nodded to music that wasn't country, but wasn't that newfangled hip-hop either. There were long tables set for a meal that hadn't arrived, and a podium where men who felt important would likely find themselves in a few hours. Tom may not have known anyone, or understood what had brought them here, but he knew what was happening all too well.

He may have more gray hair now, and his knees don't work quite like they used to, but even today, he knew just where he was the moment he walked into the building at the DW Ranch. The smiles and hand-shakes were all superficial. There was something else driving the interests of the people here. Tom knew damned well these were the kind of people who knew power and influence and desired more than anyone in the county could ever realize. It wasn't his job to stop what was happening here at the ranch, though it was his job to make sure it didn't spread.

"Sheriff! You made it!" A booming came across the barn.

It took him a couple of awkward minutes to shove his way through the crowd. When Dalton's round, bearded face showed up, Tom couldn't help but notice the smile that stretched from ear to ear like a toddler with his hand in the cookie jar. Amid the cigar and cigarette smoke filtering through the air, indecipherable chatter ringing out, bustling of people in every direction all at once, and celebratory bells of gambling mixed with excruciating groans of loss, Dalton's presence was akin to a would-be God among men.

The two clasped hands and patted the other's shoulder as if they'd been friends all their lives. When they instinctively leaned closer to exchange words, it was Tom who spoke first.

"Sure is a lot of the Hispanic variety here."

"Never change, Tom. It's what I like about you," Dalton responded, before finding a serious tone. "You're predictable."

"A lot of new faces, too."

"Don't be like that. You've met these people before, business associates, friends, friends of friends. You know how it goes. People come and go, but they all are here to help our community that we care so much about."

Tom squinted his eyes, unsure of how to respond.

"It's always a curse, running for public office. Forced to call upon the hand you aim to serve, desperate for money but unable to show your willingness to do what it takes for fear of being labeled—"

"A coward?" Tom cut him off.

"A coward is right, Sheriff."

"So, you're really gonna run for that seat at Congress?"

"I sure am."

"You know what they do to people who run for those kinds of positions, right? If you had anything meant to be private before running, it won't be private no more."

"It's just like those criminals on *COPS*, always running from the law. If you don't do nothing wrong, you ain't got nothing to hide from. Ain't that right?"

Tom looked into the eyes of Dalton and saw pure, radiating sincerity, even though he knew better than anyone else alive that it was all a lie. Dalton did have something to hide from. He was hiding it right now, behind those puppy dog eyes and masquerading in front of a multi-million dollar ranch turned into a damned circus. Despite this, Tom had no chance in hell of stopping him.

"That's right, Dalton," Tom admitted, letting his eyes fall to Dalton's feet. "I never seen you hide from anyone or anything. That's what I like about *you*."

Dalton either didn't catch his meaning, or chose to simply ignore it and responded to Tom like he'd asked a question that never truly came to mind. "You might be wondering how exactly it's our 175th event when the ranch was only just started by myself a few years ago."

"It certainly came to mind," Tom lied.

"It all goes back to my great, great, granddaddy. He always promised my great-grandaddy, who was a coal miner through and through, that one day they'd run a big ol' ranch together. They'd work beneath the blue sky instead of a black cave, they'd befriend horses and work cattle instead of running coal, and they'd make a livin' for their family doin' it, too. The DW Ranch stands today as a testament to that very promise.

"It's been 175 years since that promise was made, and after all these years, it's finally time for the ranch to give back to the community my family called home, the community that would eventually pave the way to becoming the home of the DW Ranch. That's what the benefit is—all about—giving back."

"That's nice, Dalton," said Tom, who only caught about half of the long-winded story due to the music being turned up just a little too loud.

"It also sounds a heck of a lot better than the sixth annual event or some shit!" Dalton held his hands up in fake exaggeration as he laughed at his own joke.

"You got a point there."

"Walk with me." Dalton slapped Tom on the back, his hand puffy, calloused hand forcing Tom forward from the impact. "What's happening here isn't really appropriate for the general public to see, if you get where I'm goin' with this. Now, when you start calling me Congressman Woodson, the people here are gonna start seein' all kinds of new developments and economic opportunities. You'll see my pretty smilin' face in those cheap little lawn signs on every home in the county, and I'll be a household name. That's when all this here is really gonna pay off."

"You sure it's smart to get in bed with these people?"

"I only get in bed with Mrs. Woodson, thank you very much."

"Right."

"I brought you here so you could see firsthand the

progress we're making," Dalton continued. "So that you can be a part of what is happening."

"You told me that last year, sir. You told me all of this last year. You told me the year before that, too."

"I'm glad you remember, Tom. I really am."

The two men walked through the crowd as they cheered, laughed, threw handfuls of cash into the air, and drank glass after glass of a clear liquid Tom knew better than to assume was water. It was an awkward moment to share with Dalton, and he'd just begun to wonder what the point of it all was when the dots were connected for him.

"You see that man up there?" Dalton pointed to the one in the makeshift boxing ring, getting his face clobbered. "That man crossed that man over there." This time, he pointed to another gentleman dressed in a suit with a pencil mustache and wide-brimmed cowboy hat. "He didn't remember the one thing he was never supposed to forget."

"What was that?"

Before Tom's answer could come, the man who lacked the strength to even fight back took a devastating blow to his orbital socket, and the gruesome result left the crowd visibly reeling in disgust. He wasn't missing his eye just yet, but it was damn close.

"To keep his *fuckin'* mouth shut."

"Look, sir, I appreciate the well-wishes and the reminder to not stick my nose where it doesn't belong, but we've gone through this. I'm the sheriff around here. It's my job to not just stick my nose in it, but to sniff it out then strangle it with my bare hands."

"Is that a threat?"

"Now, why would I threaten you? Especially here on your own ranch, surrounded by these fine people. I know my place, that's all I'm trying to say. And I won't forget it, either."

"You're a good man," said Dalton, before his voice faded off to be replaced by the thumping of music he could've lived with never hearing again.

Tom hoped these were the last words to be exchanged between them, and he hoped he'd get off easy in containing what was about to happen when the liquor and silver-lined words finally took hold for the night. His hopes were destined to be shattered, though.

"You might want to check on the Coleman Ranch when you leave here, by the way," said Dalton. "I'm hearing bad things."

A glint in his eye was all that remained before Dalton turned and left Tom alone, wondering if the conversation he'd just suffered was in fact real. The ranch owner forced the crowd of men he towered over out of his way without looking back. He walked slowly by rows of empty chairs set up in front of a stage with a podium centered between two eighty-inch television screens that hadn't been turned on. People were gathering around, yet to take their seat, but an auctioneer was prepping himself at the podium, warming himself up to a raucous backdrop of money-spending men. Something was gearing up, and as much as his role as sheriff would demand him to know what was happening, in his heart, he knew he wanted nothing to do with it. Tom watched Mr. Woodson until there was nothing left to see except mindless consumption, greed, lust, and desperation that filled his vision.

He might have stayed there beyond his welcome, lost in the suspicion of what was going on beneath his very nose, in his own county, that he could do nothing about. Or at least that's what Dalton believed. Tom didn't stick around as sheriff most of his life because he was terrible at his job. He was resourceful. He believed in the rule of law. But he also believed in what his own mom and pops called *karma*, and that meant it was all just a matter of time before the truth about this place would come to light. As he watched the party unfold, a gathering of the financiers of whatever underworld Dalton F. Woodson claimed to have come from, he knew he had to keep going.

His spiraling train of thought was interrupted by a vibrating in his pocket. He snapped back to reality and shoved his hand all the way up to his wrist into his jeans to find the one thing in life he hated most—his cell phone. He didn't have time to look at who was calling before he dragged his thumb against every fiber of his being to accept the call.

"Sheriff Tom," he said, to whoever it was on the other end of the line.

"Sheriff, it's me."

Tom didn't say anything. He just waited.

"It's me, O'Kelley," the man's voice came through. "We're going to hit the Coleman Ranch again tonight. The guys are saying a thousand head. Something's happening."

"Tell me something I don't know already, O'Kelley."

"We killed a guy named Adam Barnes two nights ago."

Chapter 8

Hollywood's once lucrative obsession with romanticizing the American West made it out to be a goldmine of wealth for the taking, where any man with cash in one hand and a woman in the other could lay claim to the earth and make their own way.

There was no other way to pass on the legends of the wildest frontier because the West itself demanded it to be this way. It was inhabited by larger-than-life figures who told extravagant tales about their exploits, and in doing so, gave the people exactly what they wanted to believe most. Dime novel literature and word of mouth kept them alive before films immortalized every tall tale imaginable. To be living in a world ruled by ranchers, farmers, tradesmen, a sheriff and their deputies, builders of forward progress, and the dead weight of the soulless filling every saloon simply wasn't a life that existed today. Maybe it never did. Maybe the Eastwoods and Waynes of the world told us something which could never be true. Maybe the myth of the West wasn't the romanticized life of freedom, justice, and responsibility that storytellers so often love to make it out to be.

From where Rob was sitting, he'd be the first to say such a life was made up in the heads of people who knew only concrete and convenience. He'd delivered exactly what he was told and paid the price to do it all over again. The man he'd gunned down was no different than the dream of a life in the American West —he simply never existed. There was no regret about his actions, nor fear of retribution to come. He felt only inescapable dread, sinking to the pit of his stomach, torturing him with the thought of another ghost haunting his every step.

He sat alone. A bunkhouse belonging to the Bossman himself turned out to be the only place to grab some shuteye. It just so happened to be placed on the backside of five hundred acres that just so happened to run parallel with the headquarters of Coleman Ranch. It was far from luxurious. It was closer to a hunting cabin that had been abandoned years ago. Dim yellow lighting and bedding you had to peel the moth balls out of made for a bleak outlook, especially given the approaching storm threatening them from just outside, but there wasn't much in life which couldn't be remedied by a pocket full of wadded up cash.

It was the kind of money you didn't have to ask where it came from. There were no strings, or paper trails documenting its changing of hands. It may as well have been bright and sunny beyond the walls of the bunkhouse, shining glorious light down with a promise of even brighter days ahead, because Rob and his cowboys had finally reached the one day where nothing could ever get them down—payday.

It didn't matter they had been told to take on another job that night. It didn't even matter that the job was probably ten times the size of anything they'd done before. The only thing that mattered to the men Rob rode with was they could afford the vices to soften their struggle through life for just a little bit longer.

Rob had already been through them all, though. He'd lived on violence, on addiction, on gambling, risking his ego and wielding any sense of power he could find, and all it ever did was leave him empty. Sure, he'd made plenty of money in his day, but he had nothing to show for it. He was empty deep inside. It wasn't a hole that could be filled with money or liquor, love or lust, or even friendship. It was just a void, and no matter what he did to fill it, the void did what it always did—it swallowed it up and begged for more.

As the men forced themselves to stuff their cash wherever they thought it wouldn't be stolen, they shuffled about their chores to prepare for the night ahead. Working in the rain wasn't something anyone looked forward to, but they also knew what they were up against, and tonight, it would be in their favor. The Coleman Ranch headquarters was two thousand acres of cattle country, with five hundred more of farming land, and a dozen more on top of that for the family homestead. They were the kind who could afford security, night watch crews, and insurance just in case anything slipped through the cracks. Tonight was all about getting in and out, as quick as their horses would carry them.

"I ain't carryin' all that shit this time," Sam's voice finally broke the silence. "I told you. This time, you're the one haulin' all that damn rope. You're the one keen on ropin' everything in sight anyways."

"My bags are full already, sorry, Sam."

"And what exactly do you have that's so important, Cliff?"

Rob sighed and continued to thumb through the wad of cash inside his jacket pocket, refusing to intrude on yet another argument. When Cliff started to laugh, he finally gave in and looked in their direction. Cliff had opened up his saddlebag to the sound of gently rattling brass inside the leather.

"The hell you think we're doin'? Going to war?"

"You never know," Cliff answered. "Especially after last time."

"It was *one* bullet. Stop being so dramatic, you asshole."

"What if it's more than that next time? Hell, this place is as big as a freaking college campus. Who knows what those people are packing. I ain't getting outgunned out there."

"Do you even know how to shoot?"

"Sure, I do."

"You ever been shot at?"

"I have," said Hicks.

Sam and Cliff both turned to look at Hicks, who was dead serious despite not quite understanding that he'd made himself available in the argument at hand.

"Well, Hicks, I wasn't gonna bother you, but since you insist," Sam said, as he pushed the coils of rope into Hicks' chest. "You can carry all this extra rope while Mr. *Gun Hand* over there pretends to protect us all."

Rob smirked at the new nickname bestowed upon Cliff, knowing it would be resurrected over the course of the next year enough times to cause multiple fist-fights between Sam and Cliff. He listened to their bickering continue over who carried the rope the last time, who carried more in their saddlebags, who did more work at every job, and who was the best cowboy out of the bunch, alongside anything else they could think of to piss one another off in the moment. To better pass the time, he reached into his own bag and pulled out the black leather journal that called his name more often than he'd cared to admit.

When he cracked open the yellowed and frayed pages, he flipped through the entries until he found the next page detailing yet another twisted turn of events for the original writer following their batch of stolen cattle and the dear family who paid the price.

June 6, 1881

> *We went to war today. There will be rumors of bloodshed and the heroism which prevailed. They will tell stories of a battle, of the dead, and the ones who walked away. Tall tales to be written into literature and sold for ten cents to people with nothing better to spend their money on. We returned to the cabins and are waiting until it's safe to leave. It was my brother's idea, and he sold the boss on it with ease. Twice the usual payout blinded us. We rode into the county last night, and went into town at the first light to fill our pockets as much as our saddlebags. There were homes full of women and children sitting beside candlelight shining through their windows. But there were no horses tied up in the street, and no men drunkenly stumbling from one watering hole to the next. It didn't feel right, but we pressed on. How were we supposed to know there was some kind of deputy meeting*

*going on for all the neighboring counties? We went in
firing. They returned fire. It lasted for only minutes, but
felt like days. My brother shot first, and I followed. The
boss settled the score before it was all said and done. By
the time we got smart enough to ditch the job with what
was in our pockets, half our gang was dead in the street.
It was a lot of death for only $2,000. Strange to think
this is the life that will put my name in newspapers and
novels for the world to admire. Sometimes it feels like all
we do is kill. I've learned there is more than one way to
earn a living and be remembered for it, though. Days like
this make me think maybe that governor's offer might be
worth considering…*

Bob.

The man who wrote the journal may have had a
hard life, but the troubles from the past faded from his
mind as soon as he stowed it away. There were problems of his own here and now which required his
attention. The torrent of rain coming down just
outside was chief among them. With a grunt loud
enough to stop the other cowboys in their tracks, Rob
rose to his feet and looked around.

It seemed like they all expected a rousing speech, a
word of encouragement to motivate them to do the
job they were already being paid for. This wasn't something Rob had in mind.

"It doesn't matter if it's ten head or a thousand
head, your job ain't no different. Get 'em all from one
spot to the next. We're all just asses in the saddle. The
only advice you're gonna get from me is to keep your
ass in that saddle."

"Our fearless leader," said Cliff.

"Do you even know how many we're supposed to get tonight?"

"When have I ever told you the number? You know the deal. We clean them out."

"I know where we're going, I ain't an idiot," Sam shot back. "The Colemans have been around as long as there has been a town to be around. This isn't some lease for tax exemptions or a campsite for grazing. It's the actual Coleman Ranch."

"Last I heard it was over a thousand head," Cliff said.

"I already told y'all none of that matters."

"I ain't dying over this job."

Rob turned to face Cliff and did his best to restrain the fury brewing in his belly, but was unable to control the outburst that poured out.

"If I could drag your body to the Bossman himself in exchange for my own freedom to live as I see fit, there'd be a bullet rattling around in that thick skull of yours right damn now."

Cliff just stood there.

"Until that day comes, we're gonna go out in the pouring rain and punch cattle. That means me, you, Sam, Hicks, and the dipshit back there are gonna go get it done."

"I have a—"

"Shut the hell up, O'Kelley!" each of the men's voices came in unison and all at once, like a chorus rehearsing for the sole purpose of making him feel bad.

"Do you got that?"

"I got it."

"It's time to saddle up, y'all," said Rob, locking his gaze on Cliff, who did everything he could to avoid making eye contact. "Those truckers won't wanna keep their eighteen-wheelers idling all night long."

"The what?" Sam couldn't hide his surprise, even when it was in his best interest to not say anything.

Rob didn't bother to answer. He yanked open the door to the bunkhouse and made sure to slam it loud enough on his way out to make a point. It wasn't the attitude or the complaining. It was the sacrifice being laid on Rob's shoulders. It was the burden that he alone was being told to shoulder, and it was not fair, simply put. Those men didn't care about the sacrifices he'd made. He knew as much, but when it came down to it, he didn't care about them.

Rain splattered on his jacket and across his face. It flooded the swirling thoughts of what he'd endured, and it quenched the fury rumbling deep in his belly. Thunder cracked in the distance. Flashes of lightning soon followed. There was an unmistakable attempt by the earth itself to wash away what had been.

Instead of returning to the same situation he had just escaped from, he went to find the only company he truly enjoyed. He didn't mind the hay and manure. Time spent with his horse was about the only time he would never come to regret. A feeling of dread crept over him as he planted his ass in the musty ground kept unnaturally moist by a run-down barn abandoned to the effects of time.

His horse nudged him gently on the shoulder, then again on the side of his face, knocking

off his cowboy hat to reveal disheveled hair which hadn't seen a shower in a week. He wasn't much one for talking to the beast he'd been through so much with. He always felt communication happened in a different way. There wasn't ever much of a reason to say aloud what the two were already going through together. This time, he found some use in it after all.

"It's about that time," he told the horse. Considering he never did that much talking to his horse, he never really found it necessary to give him a name, either. There was only one name that stuck after the few years they'd been together, and it was about as straightforward as possible—*horse*. "We been through a lot together, Horse. I gotta bad feelin' about what we're getting into here. Just promise me one thing…"

Horse nudged Rob on the shoulder one more time before gently shaking his head from side to side and letting out a whisper of a neigh. Rob's conviction on speaking to horses was weakened at that moment, he felt this beast was listening to him, and he owed it even the simplest form of respect in return.

"Don't run off on me when shit hits the fan," he said.

They remained in the barn in silence for several minutes. Gnats, moths, and every other kind of insect scurries about without end as the creatures of the night carried on outside the walls of the barn. It was serene. Rob could get used to such a feeling. He fought the urge to allow his mind to drift toward a possibility where he saddles up and rides away into the night to leave it all behind. Hell, he even stood up without thinking about it, as if his body would carry him away without so much as a second thought.

He forced himself to sit back down, though. As much as he wanted to run, he knew this time he couldn't. Not so soon after what he'd just done. Sure, there was a debt to be paid. But he could clear his name in a single night if the rumors of a thousand head waiting on their arrival proved to be true. There was nothing left to be done except wait on the clock to strike midnight. Once it did, they'd be off, just like the message that had come through to each of the cowboys huddled out at the bunkhouse.

It wouldn't do much good to dwell on the challenges of what was waiting for them, so instead of worrying himself sick, Rob returned his attention to the journal waiting patiently for him inside his jacket pocket. When he pried open the book, it sounded as if he tore multiple pages right out by accident. His heart jumped. He couldn't explain why it worried him so much, but he couldn't bring himself to think about having damaged it even the slightest. Much to his surprise, on closer inspection in the dim bulbs of the barn, casting more shadows than light, he realized two pages had been stuck together in the bottom corner.

"Is that…" Rob's whisper trailed off.

There was a red stain on the bottom of the page, pressed into the paper by a thumb from who knows how long ago, leaving a faint trace of a fingerprint. Rob's heart hadn't stopped fluttering yet. His eyes couldn't find the words quick enough. Trembling fingers matched his breathing as he shoved the book closer to his face and became lost in the entry.

June 5, 1881

> *My horse died today. We water them, we rest them, and we don't push them too hard when we're riding. There are few who treat their horses better than we do when we're on the run, and that's because we know better than most, if you ain't got a horse, you ain't getting far. We was moving through the canyon separating us from town, where we were told a job as big as anything we've ever done was waiting*

for us. Morale was high. We had beef and beans, coffee, and even some sugar to go with it. One guy sang while we rode. It was nice. Things went right for a few days, but they always have a way of going wrong. We stopped to water the horses like we always did a few hours after midday. This time, I didn't pay attention like I should, and when the poor thing went for a drink, the quietest rattlesnake you ever saw reached up and bit it right in the neck. It couldn't breathe through the swelling. Suffocated to death. The boys had a couple in tow, so I'll avoid being buzzard food for another day, but I liked that horse. Was even thinking of naming him. He would've been the first I'd ever named. He just stared at me, lying on his side, gasping his last breaths, and I couldn't do nothing for him. I wonder if I'll share the same look in his eye when it's finally my turn? My brother says it doesn't do much good to think about stuff like that. But it's gonna happen. Just like how I'll be famous all around the world one day. Might as well go ahead and get ready for it. When we was leaving the watering hole, one of the guys said my horse dying was a bad omen. I'm still not sure if it's true. My brother says not to think about that either. I won't tell him, but I think it could be something else. What if my horse dying is the last bad thing that ever happens to me?

Bob.

Rob shook his head after reading the final sentence. He knew what was about to happen to the man whose words carried on through time only to sink his heart. It seemed there was nothing good in store for him or the man in the journal. Rob reached up and patted Horse on the shoulder, grateful for the fact that he wouldn't have to go through something as dreadful as watching your horse die. Despite what was being asked of him, he at least took comfort in the solitude he and Horse shared in the barn together.

He finally climbed out of his own spiraling thoughts and closed the journal in his hand. What waited for him just behind the journal was enough to damn near make him pass out from fear. The rain had given a home to a four-foot-long water moccasin inching its way inside the stall.

"*Sonofabitch*," he whispered.

Chapter 9

Rob jumped first.

His extremities pulsated with adrenaline before he could understand what was happening. There was a tingle in his fingers and his toes. His hands were shaking, and his vision was blurry. Thoughts mushed together like a train wreck in the middle of a sixteen-lane highway, colliding with one another at speeds they should've never been traveling at. He reacted too slow to his own body's fight or flight instincts, and was on his feet before he could tell himself that was a stupid idea.

Horse jumped next. Not because he knew what was standing less than a foot away from his back right hoof. He jumped because Rob jumped, plain and simple. It was his mistake that set everything in motion, not anything the horse or the snake did. They were just doing the only thing they knew, they didn't have a choice. It was innate.

That was the only part Rob could relate to. He wanted to get out, to run away as fast as his legs would allow, but the water moccasin sat in his way. It was coiled up tight and pissed off. Black and brown patterns repeated throughout the length of the snake's vibrating body. The only thing Rob could focus on was its mouth, unhinged at the jaw to open far wider than what seemed natural.

If Horse had only stepped back a few more inches, his hoof would've crushed the head of the water moccasin, and everything would've been over in an instant. Rob wished with everything he had in him that hoof would go just a bit further back, but it didn't. Horse shifted uncomfortably, not knowing what was happening. Its hoof landed on the tip of the snake's tail just as Rob lost his breath, knowing what was about to come.

The snake felt the weight of the horse and lashed out immediately. It did the only thing it knew to do, the only thing nature had ever prepared it to do in such an instant. It sank its fangs into Horse's leg and closed its jaw with all the force it could muster. The venom burned on its way into Horse's bloodstream, and it kicked violently in response. Not once or twice, but over and over again, sending the water moccasin flying backward in the barn, slamming against a wooden wall with a wet *thump*. It slithered off in the opposite direction, seemingly unhurt.

Rob wouldn't know if his horse or the snake was still alive, though. By the time the snake hit the ground and his horse stopped flailing around in the stall, he was already sprinting away. He knew the nature of the snake and what his horse would do after it was bitten, but he was doing the only thing he knew to do as well. He wanted to run into the woods and never stop. He'd run until he found a bus stop, use what few bucks he had in his pocket to get him to the next town, then hobo his way out of the state of Texas, where he could leave this life behind him. He wanted to escape into the pines and oaks and yaupon, where he wouldn't care if the briar shredded his ankles and shins as he ran for freedom, and where the soundtrack of birds and cicadas could become his applause for such incredible bravery.

He wanted a lot in life, though. As was so often the case, it wasn't about what he wanted to do, it was only about what he could bring himself to do. He lacked conviction. He lacked the perseverance needed to do something so drastic. So, instead of fulfilling his deepest wishes, he returned to the bunkhouse, the place he wanted to be least in the whole world. He returned to faces of surprise, pity, anger, and anxiousness.

"It bit my horse!"

Those were the only words that came to Rob's mind. They didn't make much sense out of context, but they dang sure made sense to him. He wasn't sure what any of them could do about it, but he knew something had to be done. Not once in his moment of weakness, which saw him flee from the only real friend he'd known in his life, did he ever consider it was a life-and-death situation.

"What the hell's wrong with you, Rob?" Cliff was the first to speak.

"What bit your horse?" Sam at least pretended to care.

"Is it still out there?" Hicks asked, never one to do much else other than worry about himself these days.

"It was a water moccasin. Came right into the damned barn where my horse was. Freaked it the hell out. Next thing I know, that snake is clung onto the side of my horse's leg and won't let go. It goes flyin' in the air after the horse kicked enough times."

"What you want us to do about it?"

Rob stopped short of closing the creaky wooden door to the bunkhouse behind him. There was only blackness to be found behind him, silhouetting his presence in the door through shadows desperately trying to blot out any light from within. Raindrops fell against the aging wood and rusted tin overhead. It was a solemn night, one that matched the feeling of the cowboys inside, preparing for a job nobody knew could be pulled off. What they didn't expect was their de facto leader to come bursting into the building, yelling something about a snake biting his horse.

Rob could see confusion on their face, and in that moment, he questioned even his own sanity. What exactly could they do about it? He wasn't even sure why he ran to them, the only thing he truly remembered was the simple fact that he had to run. By the time it came down to it, the only thing left to do was to go right back where he'd escaped to find out if his horse was all right.

"Nothing," he finally said, before slamming the door to the bunkhouse closed once again to save himself from facing the embarrassment he felt.

His walk back to the barn was worse than the first time. He wanted to leave, but he couldn't. He wanted to shrink away from any sense of responsibility, but he couldn't. He wanted more than anything to never have to walk back into that bunkhouse and face the men who he was forced to work alongside, but he knew he needed them if he ever wanted to get out of the Boss-man's grip. That's all any of this was about—being done. The longer it was postponed or outright denied, the longer he'd be forced to come to terms with his own reckoning. It was unfair, the fact that he'd be the only one to be held accountable for the death of the ranch owner, but his life had never been fair to him.

That was just how Bossman worked, though. He could save you from just about any fate if you were desperate enough to avoid it. He could pull strings no one even knew existed, make crimes disappear, and charges long forgotten. But everything came at a cost. Deep down, he knew every man back inside that bunkhouse had their own demons standing between them and the Bossman, but those weren't his problems to deal with. Rob's problems were of his own making. There was a debt to be paid, and he had no choice but to pay in full. Every misstep along the way was nothing more than a tax aimed at putting him just a little more in debt and working just a little longer.

Rob was feeling the pressure of what was being asked of him and the cowboys. The Coleman Ranch headquarters was nothing like the ranchettes they'd hit along the way. They all knew it. The only thing Rob could do was avoid thinking about the catastrophe soon to come when they rode into those pastures to confiscate a thousand head of cattle and dispose of them before anyone could notice.

As he approached the barn, ignoring the job ahead turned out to be easier than he'd ever expected. The first thing he saw was the hooves splayed out across the chipped and stained concrete flooring. He already knew what happened, deep down. There were just some things in life that couldn't be believed until it simply couldn't be denied. This was something he'd do everything in his power to deny until the scent of death could no longer be ignored.

His horse was lying in the stall he'd left him in, dead as dead could ever get.

If he didn't know any better, Rob would've sworn there was a tear crawling down his cheek as he stared at the still-twitching corpse of old Horse. He didn't deserve the fate that waited for him in that musty old barn. He deserved to be retired beneath a mountain somewhere, turned out to never work beneath a saddle again, to roam the pastures and drink from creeks until age would no longer allow it. Whether it was the toxins or the stress, his horse had suffered a terrible death, and even worse—he had to do it alone.

When Horse needed him the most, Rob was running in the other direction as fast as he could.

As he stared into oblivion itself and became lost in what could have been, a distant swirling of a voice that was not his came through, muffled and distorted. It annoyed him at first. It promised to steal any sense of peace he could ever hope to find with what had happened. Most would never feel such remorse for a creature as simple as a horse, but in his line of business, it wasn't just a tool or a means to an end. They had put more hours than he'd like to count into their work together. With Horse coming to such an untimely end, all he could want in life was a simple damn second to put himself back together, to collect the pieces of himself that had shattered in his own cowardice. He'd been face-to-face with death countless times before, but those were just people, and they didn't matter. His horse was his friend—he mattered.

The voice started up again, this time sending his stomach into a flurry of anger that rolled and toiled within his insides. His eyes stayed fixed on the dead horse in the stall. The voice lingered behind him, urging him on even though he'd have nothing to do with it. It grew louder in the back of his mind. It kept growing. He couldn't run from this one, as much as he wanted to. It became the only nuisance he'd ever wanted to strangle the life out of with his bare hands.

"Boss!"

The voice was inescapable. Rob's face turned red, his belly burned white hot, his fingers trembled, and his vision closed in. He still remained fixated on the dead horse in the stall.

"Boss! You ain't gonna want to miss this!"

He could hear the voice now, make out its words, and even the direction it was pelting him from.

"Boss! Come here!"

Even the thought of turning to leave Horse again was enough to make him grit his teeth. He'd already ran once before, and now that his horse was dead, it didn't matter if he did it again. Except this time, for a reason he couldn't explain, he just didn't want to.

"Son of a bitch. Boss! Boss!"

"You know I ain't the *goddam* boss 'round here, you stupid mother fu—" Rob turned as he screamed, but his jaw dropped at what he saw behind him. There were two children, no older than ten, standing in front of Sam, who had them gripped by the collar of their shirts like they had just gotten in trouble for fighting at school. Their faces were stained with dirt and tears, and their clothes were torn, but the look in their eyes had endured something else entirely.

"It's a bunch of kids back there. Like half a dozen or so. They come runnin' out of the woods behind the bunkhouse like a bunch of maniacs. They won't say nothing, though."

The overwhelming need to dwell on his horse's death faded away into the night, washed away by the drops of rain splashing against his face. It was no longer misting. The rain came down on him like a bucket of water to the face after a whiskey-filled all-nighter.

Falling back into reality with every step forward, Rob approached the two children who couldn't bring themselves to look away from him. He didn't know what to say. He didn't know what to ask. For reasons neither he nor Sam could explain, one of the children was the first to speak, and the words that came out of his mouth formed a sentence that someone of his age should ever be forced to utter.

"Just shoot us if ya gotta, mister," the boy said. "We ain't goin' back there."

Chapter 10

"There ain't no way in hell we're taking those kids with us."

"I don't see any other choice."

"You don't? Really? Just look at 'em. They're all messed up in the head, like they got their brains scrambled."

"You think it's drugs?"

"It's something."

"We can't just leave them. Can we?"

"You really think any of us are qualified to take care of one child, much less six of 'em?"

"Probably not."

"I say we point 'em in the direction of the Coleman home, say good luck, and use the distraction to our advantage."

"These kids have been used enough."

"If you ask me, we should call the cops."

"Shut up, Hicks."

"No one asked you, Hicks."

The argument had gone in circles for about half an

hour at this point, with none of the cowboys able to find anything that resembled a consensus about the handful of kids who just showed up at the bunkhouse. Only one would speak, the rest just stared with blank looks, huddling as close to one another as possible. It was a grim situation any way the cowboys cut it. Even though it was going through each of their minds, no one dared utter the words that they had all escaped from something deep within the land owned by their own boss. Refusing to even consider what such a fact meant, seemed to be the only thing they could find an agreement on.

The biggest problem they faced wasn't the runaway children or even what they were running from, though. It was time. They were supposed to leave in the next half hour, and there were several truckers hauling in empty trailers approaching. None would be all too eager to sit around and wait while they dealt with this new problem.

It wasn't something Rob could explain with his words, but somewhere deep down in his belly, he knew it was wrong to leave the kids to their own fate. They'd gone through something he didn't even understand, by people he didn't even know. His chest hurt as the thoughts about what happened to them swirled in his head.

Sweat beaded up on his eyebrow as he shrank away from the argument of his outfit. A single drop ran down the side of his forehead from beneath the leather band inside his cowboy hat. His teeth clenched tight enough to grind in his ears. He was experiencing a more visceral reaction than he'd ever anticipated. Despite the pleas of both Sam and Cliff, and ignoring Hicks' more absurd ideas, Rob had a feeling he wasn't all too familiar with. It crept inside him and stayed hidden in his own thoughts, but it was all too thrilled to show its face when he expected it least.

Empathy wasn't exactly a virtue he was known for. More often than not, anytime a situation required him to put himself in another person's shoes, he could only bring himself to wonder how fast those shoes would carry him in the other direction, and how far he could go. His heart rate was higher than it should have been. There was a tension in his neck that usually only made itself known when he was being followed by the police for a few minutes too long. He wasn't one to be subject to panic attacks, but he'd be lying if he said he wasn't worried that he was currently getting familiar with one. He could feel his heart beating out of his chest, and his palms were itching, sweating, and tingling all at once. His throat was lodged, and his breathing was shallow. He knew he'd be forced to act one way or another, and the thought alone seemed to shut his entire body down.

When most people black out, it means collapsing to the floor in a complete state of unconsciousness. There have been many people who have succumbed to such darkness only to wake up beneath the fluorescent light of a hospital, and some who never wake up again. That isn't what happened to Rob. One minute, he was arguing about what to do with the batch of kids who stumbled onto their bunkhouse, and the next, he was on top of a horse he didn't know, riding beneath the shining stars of a clear Texas night sky, totally unaware of how he got there.

The rise and fall of his saddle lulled him back into reality as if he were falling weightlessly back into his own body. It was a narrow saddle, and it didn't allow his ass to sink deep like he preferred, and even the horn seemed cheap and useless. The reins in his hand were too small, and the stirrups made his feet point outward like he was a child riding a pony. All he could bring himself to think about was how uncomfortable he was, how his posture was all wrong, and how he even ended up on the horse he was riding.

When his memories finally started to flood back into him, Rob first thought of the death of his horse. He remembered seeing the panicked fear of facing death in Horse's eye, and he remembered how fast he ran from it all.

Then, he remembered the children, and his heart fell to his stomach.

"It ain't like we left 'em for dead."

"Their parents probably think they're already dead."

"What if it was their parents who were doing that to them?"

Rob listened to the conversation without drawing attention to himself. He tightened his grip on the resin and did his best to do the same to his own sanity.

"It's like they had their tongues cut out or some shit."

"Can't imagine what they've been through."

"They'll be fine until we get back to the bunkhouse and figure everything out."

Rob perked up. His heart finally began to rise from the pit of his stomach.

"We got bigger problems on our hands right now."

"Yeah, like a thousand of 'em."

Rob found his place to interject and resume his control of the situation and his outfit.

"No different than a hundred head, boys," he said.

"Oh, look, he does talk," the new guy, O'Kelley, somehow felt confident enough to speak up.

Rob ignored him. "A place like this, there's a heck of a lot more than a thousand head grazing. They're gonna be up in the north pastures this time of the year. Won't be hard to find. And the Colemans run black cows, no different than everywhere else, so they'll pretty much run themselves. Now stop acting like this will be anything other than another night. We get in, we punch cattle no different than we always do, and we fill those damn trailers."

"Those other places didn't have armed men riding around in the middle of the night," said Cliff.

Rob turned to make eye contact with him, allowing his glare to say everything he wanted to yell right at him.

"Except for that time, of course," he tried to cover for himself.

Even though it seemed like nothing was going to plan so far, Rob knew they were right on time. As the moonlight caused shadows in the darkness to climb over the tree line and the sweet scent of fertilized hayfields began to grow, it was only a matter of time before they could all get back to doing what they did best. There was nothing else on Rob's mind. He was in debt. And it wasn't often when they were called with an offer to damn near wipe it out.

They were lucky everything had gone as smoothly as it had, all things considered. The children's appearance was nothing more than a speed bump in the grand scheme of things. With the stars to light their path and the payout ahead larger than it had ever been before, things were looking up for Rob and his outfit.

It was all going to plan, until the first bullet was fired.

There was a whizzing sound tearing through the air, followed by the most deafening *boom* any of them had ever heard. Before anyone had a chance to react, another rang out, and a spatter of dirt flew into the air only a few feet from where Rob stood. Whatever horse he was riding on was either too slow to react or too stupid. Another *boom* cracked through the air, and this time, a bullet lodged right into a saddlebag thrown over the backside of Hick's horse.

"Nope! Hell with this," Hicks hollered, before yanking on the reins to turn his horse around. He couldn't see the blood beginning to run down his horse's rear leg, but he didn't need to in order to understand that death was on their trail.

"We didn't even make it a hundred acres in, and they're already shooting? How did they know we'd be here?" Sam was shouting in Rob's direction, but there was no time for talking.

"Find some cover, you dumbasses!"

Rob heeded his own warning and turned his horse back the way they came. They had just come through to the other side of a tree line a few minutes before, so as far as he knew, the oaks and pines and cypress would be their best bet. The hard part would be making it there alive. He'd assumed his own retreat to the woods would be signal enough for his guys to follow. He was wrong.

Hicks decided it best to race in whatever direction he could manage to steer his horse in. Bullets seemed to follow Hicks with every step, sending clouds of dirt and grass flying into the air just behind their trail. The horse managed to get fifty yards before the bullet wound in its hindquarters finally caught up to it. It started as just a simple limp, but within seconds, the horse was only searching for a patch of earth it deemed acceptable to lie down and die in.

Rob could hear the frightened shouting from Sam and Cliff. They were doing everything they could to get Hicks to come back the way he came so they could get him to safety. Rob knew better than to look back. It was a moment he knew would become a lifelong nightmare every night when he closed his eyes, but he did it anyway. Rob turned his head just in time to see everything go to hell in a handbasket.

Hicks was in the process of swinging one leg over the saddle as he dismounted the wounded horse when the bullet with his name on it struck him. It was something torn from the most violent scenes of Hollywood's imagination. The bullet entered through his right ear and exited his neck just below the jawline on the other side of his head, carrying with it all the blood, muscle, bone, and flesh that dared stand in its way, turning the last breath of Hicks into a spray of gruesome mist into the night air. His body collapsed on top of his horse in an instant.

Sam and Cliff abandoned their pleas immediately. The pasture they found themselves in fell into silence for a haunting few seconds as Hicks succumbed to the cold hands of death beneath the starry sky. Rob knew there was nothing they could do, but hoped they would come to their senses with enough time to flee for their own lives. The memory of Hicks' eyes realizing he was dying was already burned into Rob's brain and lodged in his throat, making it impossible to breathe. He couldn't holler for Sam and Cliff.

Rob turned his head one more time, just a few

paces away from the tree line, to find O'Kelley right on his heels, spurring his horse faster and faster. Wind rushed against his face, and the swell of the tree limbs overhead made it difficult to hear anything else. O'Kelley was trying to say something to him, but he didn't care. His eyes searched the horizon behind tears threatening to well up and obscure his vision even more. Shit was hitting the fan, and he knew deep down he'd watch every one of his cowboys take bullets to the head before he'd subject himself to such a fate. For now, he could only fight the urge to bail on them all, but he had to try to help them even if not a single ounce of him wanted to do such a thing.

A bullet slammed into a giant white oak just as Rob passed behind it for cover. Splinters shot out in every direction just as another bullet whizzed by with a threatening whistle into the brush behind them. He pushed his back against the oak and felt the limbs wedge into his back. His hands were trembling furiously as he fumbled at the reins, trying his best to tie the horse up out of harm's way. He tugged at the revolver on his hip, knowing all too well it wouldn't do him any good, but feeling inexplicably better with its weight in his hand.

His first shot was blind and loud and disorienting all at once. The revolver cried out with enough force to leave his ears ringing. It was a .357 magnum, and it meant business. A muzzle blast made of flame and gunpowder residue spewed forth only inches from his face as Rob returned fire. It wasn't until after he fired that he remembered he should have been calling for Sam and Hicks to find their way to him.

He pulled the revolver to his chest as the trail of smoke wafted up into his nose from the end of the barrel. It was a horrifying distraction from the gun fight unfolding, and one he'd have to ignore if he hoped to get out with his life. Rob poked his head around the corner of the tree and immediately found Sam and Cliff hauling ass in his direction. Either due to ignorance or inexperience, he stepped out from behind the tree and began waving them down, flagging their hideout for any gunmen trying to find them in the process.

Sam and Cliff were both screaming at the top of their lungs, but between the gunfire still ringing out in the distance and the pounding of Rob's heart in his chest, he couldn't make out a word they were saying. The fear in their voices carried across the wind, but their words of warning were lost entirely.

It was mumbling at best for a tedious few seconds, but as the drumming of the hooves from their horses thundered toward him, Rob was finally able to pick out a few words.

"Just run!" Sam screamed.

"There's too many of 'em!" Cliff joined in. "Go! Go! Go!"

Bullets silhouetted them as they kicked and spurred their horses to run faster. It was a torrent of screams, hooves, and bullets all swallowed in the shroud of night, rushing toward Rob at a blinding pace. He saw a Remington painting take shape before his eyes, a vision of the Wild West no one wants to believe was real, fueled by a fever dream he could never wake up from. It was obscene, and it twisted his stomach, but this time, running wasn't an option. If he ran now, he'd be gunned down just like poor Hicks was. Such a fate wasn't one he wanted to share with that man.

Sam could still grip the reins, and his head leaned

forward to ride like a man should. He was racing in a straight line as fast as his horse would allow, and he was leaving Cliff behind in a hurry. Sam had one hand up, gripping the top of his cheap, ill-fitting cowboy hat, saving it out of pure instinct. He was locked on the tree line, but his mouth was wide open as he shouted the same word over and over.

It was the one word playing over and over in Rob's mind, and it was all he wanted to do. There was an urge deep in his bones to throw in the towel and tuck his tail. It didn't matter if it would mean his immediate death. Rob felt the word fill his body, and he fought to embrace it with everything he had. *Run. Run. Run.*

"Run!" Sam screamed as he got nearer to Rob.

Cliff was a living example as to why Rob wanted to run so badly. The gunmen of Coleman Ranch had found their mark once again when taking aim at Cliff. He was holding his stomach with his dominant hand, white knuckling the reins with the other, and bellowing every cuss word that came to mind as his horse struggled to keep up with Sam's speed. All Rob could focus on was the color red. It was consuming Cliff, becoming him.

Sam reined his horse around the tree Rob was taking cover behind, his eyes wider than Rob had ever seen them before. His mouth was open, but all he could say was the word *run.* He managed to get it out one more time before he was interrupted by the voice of O'Kelley.

"Take this, ya bastards!"

Boom. Boom. Boom.

Sam whipped his head around to see O'Kelley firing a 12-gauge pump shotgun at random. It had a night sight installed where the old bead used to be, amounting to a glowing green warning before pure hellfire erupted with every shot.

"They're too far away for buckshot, dipshit!"

"Birdshot," was the word that came back from O'Kelley between blasts.

Rob joined without thinking, firing two more rounds from his revolver in the direction Cliff was riding from. There were only two left, but he had lost count after the first shot. He always knew he should've trained like everyone told him, or at the very least, gone to a range at least once. The recoil, the blast back, the deafening roar, all on top of the surge of adrenaline flowing through his extremities, was more than he could handle.

When Rob looked back behind him, Sam was already riding off into the brush, still yelling the same word over and over. But Cliff had taken his place, and he looked worse for wear. The color had left his face, seemingly leaked out of a hole in his gut. He couldn't stop grasping at the wound. Rob watched him struggle to keep conscious as he held his stomach, doing everything he could to keep his insides from falling out. He was a mess of blood, and so was his horse. Rob's stomach went to his throat as soon as they made eye contact. They both knew right then and there—Cliff wasn't making it out alive.

"Don't look so down," said Cliff. "Don't hurt much anymore. I'm just tired, is all."

"I'm sorry, Cliff. I'm so sorry."

"You might as well follow Sam out of here."

"You can come with me. We'll get you help."

"Nice try."

O'Kelley's shotgun continued to blast out behind them, mixed with spurts of swearing and short pauses to jam more rounds in the tube. It was met with rifle shots cracking out over the hill, echoing in the distance before a bullet came slamming into a tree or passing through the brush less than a second later.

"Just go," Cliff repeated himself, staring out over the horizon with heavy eyelids due to blood loss. "Get out of here."

"O'Kelley!" Rob ignored Cliff's demands. "We gotta get!"

"No shit!"

Another bullet rocketed between them, snapping branches and lodging into a pine tree no more than fifteen feet away.

"Be my guest!" O'Kelley smarted off before getting back to spraying shotgun shots into the pasture ahead, hoping to pepper their attackers enough to send them running.

They were only met with more gunfire. It sounded like a firecracker popping off in the distance, a split second before a rain of bullets came down on the woods. More people were showing up, and time was running out. Gunpowder singed Rob's nostrils, and he kept scaling his thigh with the revolver still clutched in his hand. A metallic tingle soon turned his nose upward as he caught a whiff of Cliff's current state.

He afforded the man who'd been in the outfit longer than him a pity-filled glance. Cliff was looking down at his own life pouring out of the hole in his stomach, coming to terms with the inevitable. It would be impossible to find peace in the nightmare that had become their life, but Rob could see Cliff was damned determined not to die without a fight.

Cliff raised his hand and fired three consecutive shots from a small-caliber six-shooter he always kept tucked away in his waistband. It would do no harm to those opening fire on their position, but it sure made him feel better. He paused for only a second before unloading the final three rounds across the pasture.

Rob raised his gun once again, this time handing it over to Cliff, who accepted it with an eager smirk. O'Kelley was only a second behind him, somehow appearing at his side to hand over the shotgun to Cliff.

"It's got five more rounds," said O'Kelley.

"I think there's some left in mine." Rob did his best.

"I ain't sayin' goodbye to you assholes," Cliff said, with a forced smile washing across his face.

He straightened his posture, acting like he wasn't bleeding to death, and returned his gaze to the horizon. With Rob's revolver tucked in his waist and O'Kelley's shotgun tucked into his shoulder, he steadied his horse for one final stand. Before he jammed his boot heels into his horse's side, he turned his head to Rob and spoke calmly.

"This was a trap," he said. "Find the snake and cut off his head."

With those final words, he bolted out of the tree line into the pasture, his howls of death carrying through the wind like a wraith armed with the same guns that won the West. The wails of Cliff's weapons were the last thing Rob heard as he rode away to save his own life.

Chapter 11

"Two thirty-six bid-now-bidder-bid-now two thirty-seven."

"Yup!"

"Now-give-me two thirty-eight, dollar-dollar-dollar-dollar."

"Yah!"

"Got him. Two forty! Will ya give me two forty now-now-now-give-me two forty."

"I like coming here," said Sheriff Turpin, his voice kept low and his gaze locked on the auctioneer rambling behind a podium.

"Now-give-me two forty-five, two forty-five, two forty-five. I got two forty-four over here. Gotta give me two forty-five. Give me two forty-five."

"Ay!"

"Two forty-six! It's a fine number, but I know a finer one too."

"This whole shindig has been goin' on a heck of a lot longer than any of us has been alive. Used to be the nicest place in town, the place where all the money was made for some, and all of it was spent for everyone else."

"Two forty-seven, two forty-seven. Give me two forty-seven dollar-dollar-dollar two forty-seven now-now-now."

"It was the heartbeat of the industry that put food on the table for every family in a hundred-mile radius."

"Two forty-seven? Two forty-seven?"

"This was the place where you would make it or break it."

"Sold! Two forty-six a pound."

"Sure ain't the nicest place in town anymore," said O'Kelley.

The calves that jittered and scrambled through the half-circle pen covered in shavings were pushed out only seconds later by two prod-wielding men too scared to come out from behind their steel gates to make much of a difference. The calves were smart enough to find their own way out, and a new batch made their way in. These new calves were red and white marked Herefords, purebred from the looks of them, and the auctioneer did nothing to hide his excitement. Chants and jokes came from behind the podium as bidders prepared to make themselves known.

The Panola sale barn had now become a place of necessity. It wasn't run down quite yet, especially compared to what other counties were dealing with, but it was sure getting there. Rafters were barely holding on, covered almost entirely by cobwebs and dust. Stadium-style bleachers made of wood at least a hundred years old were barely usable, worn down by the same asses planted in them week after week for years and years and years. To anyone with an untrained nose, it reeked of manure and urine, but the men and women inside the sale barn could pick out the bitterness of the coffee at everyone's side and the sweet smell of money either coming into their wallets or leaving it.

Tom knew O'Kelley didn't have any clue why they met at such a place. He probably thought it was obscure enough for no one to look, or loud enough where no one could overhear what they had to talk about. Either way, he'd be dead wrong. Tom came every week to do something more than catch up on small talk about the weather and the historic prices of pairs.

"Still a lot of truth to be found in a place like this, though," Tom said, as the bidding got started once again. "Every Thursday, the most tried and true people you ever met come to this place to make their fortune or risk it all. If there's one thing I've learned about coming here every week for the past few years, it's that you can't sneak nothing by them."

O'Kelley turned to look at Tom, studying his face and doing his best to find anything in his expression that would give away his true intent. There was nothing to be found. Tom was as stoic as they make them when he wanted to be. His eyes were locked on the auctioneer, darting down to the calves every so often.

"Guy down there on the front row." Tom motioned to a man as old as the dirt in the rafters, with suspenders falling from his shoulders and a cowboy hat that was probably worn on back in the 1970s. "A couple weeks ago, they ran a couple six-hundred-pound steers in, numbers just kept climbing higher and higher. I could see something didn't sit right with the old man, and sure as I'm sitting with you right now, he stood up and grabbed one of those steers by the ear and got to hollerin'. There was an implant stuck in its head, something that can't be done before slaughter."

"What did they do?"

"They listened to him. Checked the ears and sure enough, they each had an implant jammed into the skin on their ear. Had just healed up, probably a few days before they got dropped off to sell. They kicked them out right then and there."

"You trying to say I'm like that old man? Telling on someone so no one gets cheated?"

"I'm saying this is a place you can trust. Ain't got nothing to do with you, unless you want it to be about you."

"I don't."

"You know why I come here?"

O'Kelley didn't answer immediately. He shifted uncomfortably in the bleacher and watched the cattle rush into the pen to be put on display for the buyers and sellers in the dimly lit crowd, then get pushed out just a few minutes later. When he finally decided to speak up, he was about as far from the right answer as he could have imagined.

"It's the one time in your life you ain't surrounded by criminals?"

"You're smarter than they give you credit for," said Tom. "But no, that's not it."

"You got me."

"I ain't never seen a single head of cattle stolen from the ranches y'all raid come through that pen there." Tom pointed his wrinkled, curled index finger at the pen in front of them. "Not a single time. All you people steal and steal and steal, and the only place in the county you can sell at hasn't seen any of your faces a single time. It's not just here either. Shelby County, Rusk, San Augustine, Sabine, hell even way up north in Cass County, there ain't a sale barn out there that has seen hide nor hair of you people."

"I don't see how you keep up with it all." O'Kelley shook his head as he realized why they were at the sale barn.

"Just gotta see it, that's all."

The auctioneer was one of a kind, carrying on a backdrop of words flowing like raindrops in a storm, broken up only by the occasional offhand comment. He knew just about everyone in the sale barn by their first name, and he took advantage of it to sell every calf that came in front of him.

Tom and O'Kelley were sitting side by side, with their boots propped up on the empty bleacher in front of them. They were tucked up in a corner, mostly by themselves, and they didn't do much to mask their voices or hide their faces. It was one of several meetings Tom had arranged with O'Kelley, and they typically covered the same topics in every meeting.

Who they hit last. Who was being hit next. How much they'd taken. Who was being talked to. What was being said. Basically, every detail O'Kelley could think of during his time with the rustling outfit striking all over East Texas. That is what was expected each and every time. Most of the information was repeated every meeting, but it was unconditional if O'Kelley hoped to get out of his sentence without serving any more time than he already had. Tom knew someone in his position could never be trusted, but he also knew all too well that there were too few who could survive such an occupation for too long. One way or another, the situation would simply sort itself out.

"Now it's my turn," said O'Kelley. "You know why I keep showing up to these damned meetings?"

"Because you have to."

"Because I want to survive my sentence. Do you get that? I don't want to die in some jail cell. I don't want to die by the hand of some lifer with nothing better to do that day. And more than anything, I don't want to die out in some random pasture running away from a bunch of rifle-toting rednecks too drunk to care about gunning someone down for shits and giggles."

"I'm not sure I'm following," said Tom.

"You're not? Let me catch you up to speed here. I told you about us going into the Coleman Ranch headquarters, told you about how many head we were lookin' for, and I even told you down to the very hour when we'd be making our pass."

"I remember."

"So, do you remember tipping off those gun hands about all that stuff I told you?"

"That part I don't remember."

"Well, that's just real convenient, because someone knew we were coming. They were waiting on us, and they damn sure didn't wait to start shooting. I watched a guy get his neck blown out from a bullet he never saw comin' his way."

Tom decided it was best not to answer. He knew what it was like to watch a man die, but he also knew the man sitting across from him carried his own demons and cared nothing for ones as old as the sheriff's.

"You know what the hell that is like? Of course you don't. You drive around in your little clown car and sit at sale barns staring at stickers on their asses pretending to do detective work. Meanwhile, I'm out there doing the real work on top of all that cowboy shit you put me up to."

"Don't get lost in all that now, boy," Tom finally spoke up. "You know what you signed up for, and you know what it'll get you if everything goes right. Just shut up and smile a little bit longer, and we'll pin the tail on the real jackass."

"We already know who's doing this, so why can't you just go haul him in?"

"Why would I tell you anything? You need to be telling me shit. So, get to it."

A bull weighing well over fifteen hundred pounds came stomping into the half-circle pen, kicking up shavings and snorting as he entered. His size elicited the same audible response from the onlookers as the auctioneer. He was broad and muscled, hidden against the sleekness of his dark coat. He was an over-whelming void of blackness, trouncing back and forth, getting more pissed off by the second.

The auctioneer wasted no time in indulging the wishes of the old men and women who were all too eager to spend money they didn't have for a herd sire they simply didn't need. A bull like that was hard to resist, though. When the auctioneer picked up his rambling at the same pace he left off, hands flew up, and the numbers kept climbing.

"I just thought the first thing you needed to know was that I almost got gunned down because *someone* tipped the Coleman Ranch off to what we were doing. I know it was you, and I want you to know I don't appreciate you trying to get me killed. That's bullshit and you know it is."

"You done?"

"It's a shame you did it, too, because we were gonna meet the Bossman on the drop off."

"Now, *that's* bullshit."

"It's true. There was some big event we were supplying and rumor was we were gonna share a drink with the man to celebrate. Ain't no celebrating going on now, though."

"There never should have been," said Tom. "That big event you were talking about? I was at it. And I won't tell you everything, since the flow of information should always be from you to me, but it's worth mentioning there was enough cartel leaders there to declare the place an active warzone."

"Hell," O'Kelley sighed. "You shoulda turned it into one."

Tom finally broke his gaze on the auction still playing out in front of him. The bull filled up the entirety of the pen, jumping back and forth, searching for a weakness where thousands of others just like it never could. He allowed himself to think about the inevitability of passing through the pen. There was something divine about the passing of fate, about finding out what it had in store for you in the reflection of the eyes of others. He sat in the audience of life-and-death.

"I did call a few favors to those guys out at Cole-man's," Tom admitted. "I had to do something to stop whatever was going on out there. I didn't do it to kill you, either. If my life has taught me one thing worth remembering, it's that people like you are never told to pay the toll. It always comes for more good people than bad, but you people always find a way of sneaking by untouched."

"I don't know if I should take that as a compliment or not."

"Take it however you want. It don't do me any good to say those men you watched get all shot up out in some guy's pasture gave their lives for nothing more than a short delay."

"Sold!" The auctioneer shouted to unknowingly punctuate what Tom was trying to explain. "Mr. Coleman, thank you as always for your generosity and mighty deep pockets."

The joke elicited a brief chuckle from most in the audience, except for O'Kelley. His jaw was slack, and he couldn't take his eyes off the elderly man with graying, curly hair tucked beneath a worn-out black felt cowboy hat. Tom couldn't help but let out a chuckle of his own. The timing was just about perfect, but O'Kelley sniffed it out. Tom had brought him here to humiliate him, sure, but also to make a point.

"The world will always continue on. Don't matter who gets killed," Tom explained. "Best thing we can do is make sure it's the right people who get killed. That way, the rest of us can have a chance at some sense of decency in the world."

"You are one cruel son of a bitch" said O'Kelley.

"It's the world that's cruel, son. After what you've been through, I'm not quite sure how you haven't learned that yet."

"That's where you're wrong. I've known the world for what it is since before you and I ever crossed paths. Don't nothing surprise me anymore. That's how I stay alive, too. You do what you gotta."

"So, you wouldn't be surprised to learn Mr. Coleman down there woke up to fifteen hundred missing cattle and two bodies being dragged out of the woods, then?"

O'Kelley was speechless. Tom watched the horror in his eyes turn to something else. Betrayal washed across his face, flushing the color from his cheeks before giving way to a scornful stare.

"We were a fuckin' distraction," he said, more to himself than anything else.

"You were. And I did nothing to stop what was happening."

"Hicks and Cliff died for nothing."

"They don't have to."

"You just said it yourself, there ain't nothing we can do."

"There is something you can do, it's why we keep having these meetings. You think I just like lookin' at your ugly ass face?"

"Women love this face, you know," O'Kelley said, as he reached up and touched his own cheek, fighting the urge to find a mirror to confirm a suspicion Tom had created out of nowhere. "And there ain't nothing I can do, especially now. I've told you everything I know. We haven't been given another job yet, and no one is even speaking to each other. It's just radio silence on my end."

"There's something you haven't told me yet. I don't know what it is, but there's something."

O'Kelley gave it consideration. The calves continued to rush in and rush out through the sale barn as the morning dragged on. Tom watched the man next to him become lost in his own thoughts. His informant grew distant, refused to speak, much less make eye contact with him. Tom may have been playing a hunch with his comment, but in that moment, he knew there was something else he had to pry out.

As luck would have it, he wouldn't have to do much prying at all. O'Kelley opened up suddenly, and every word hurt him more than the last.

"There were some kids," he said.

"What the hell does that mean?"

"It means there were some kids," O'Kelley repeated. "We were waiting out at the bunkhouse butted up to the south side of the Coleman Ranch. Everyone was standing around with their thumb up their asses waiting until go time, when all of a sudden a handful of little kids come running up from behind the bunkhouse out of the trees."

"Teenagers up to no good?"

"More like ten-year-olds runnin' for their lives."

"You should've started with this, dumbass."

"They didn't do anything worth talkin' about. We sent 'em to the Coleman's headquarters, the opposite direction we were planning on goin', and went about our business."

"Did they say anything? Their names? What happened to them?"

"Now, I wasn't payin' attention quite like I should have," O'Kelley admitted. "But I'm pretty sure they said something about not goin' back somewhere."

"My God!"

"What?"

"Y'all were on his property, not the Coleman's, right?"

"Yes, sir."

"Did they look malnourished? Like they hadn't bathed in days? Were they too scared to talk?"

"Well, they didn't look like they were dressed in

their Sunday best, if that's what you're asking. Only one of the kids said anything, if I remember right. The rest of 'em kind of just stood there and looked at us."

"That son of a bitch," Tom whispered through his teeth.

"You gonna tell me something now?"

"Those children were victims, O'Kelley. That man you work for is doing more for the cartel than any of us had ever imagined."

Chapter 12

July 4, 1881

    The governor keeps writing. He has more cash in one fist than anything we've been able to scrounge up over the last four weeks. It isn't my first time getting letters with promises no one could ever dare to keep. Between the money dangling in front of me and the trail of blood behind me, it seems my days writing history books with gunpowder and lead are coming to an end. It was sooner than I'd ever hoped for. The offer comes into my mind on nights like this, even when I know it shouldn't. The men are fighting, and there is no end in sight. My brother does not have the patience of most sane men. By the time the arguing grew too loud to ignore, he had already drawn his pistol. I would never tell him I agreed with their sentiments, lest a bullet find the back of my head as well, but surely they know we are not winning this self-appointed war. Our life on the run has its days numbered. My brother doesn't seem to believe it, however. The first man who told him otherwise was staring down the barrel of his Peacemaker in a matter of seconds. My brother and my boss laughed when the gun cried out, but no one else did. It was a warning to the rest of us, a sign of what was to come if we faltered in our loyalty. It makes me think of what the governor had to offer. It makes me think of what story my own pages of history could tell. Getting shot in the back of the head may not be an honorable end, but it was at least mercy. I wouldn't want to look the man in the eyes before I took him out of this world. When I watched my brother gun down that man who'd fought by our side time and time again, I wondered if he lacked the moral standing to look him in the eyes as well. No matter what happens, I fear such an end awaits us all.

Bob.

Aging leather and brittle pages gave off a familiar scent. It was the only welcoming part of Rob's return from the failed job at the Coleman Ranch. He wasted no time in opening the old journal and throwing himself into the scribbled cursive handwriting from another time and place, far from his own screwed up life choices.

As his eyes scanned through every sentence, crawling through every word and fixating on every letter, his brain began to connect pieces that were not there in reality. A switch was flipped somewhere in him. It couldn't be explained, but his gut swirled with a fiery curiosity that refused to be ignored. His hand was already in his pocket, fiddling around before he could consider the implications of his own conspiracies. When he produced the tiny, torn piece of paper that had stayed wadded up in his pocket for years and years, his heart stopped.

It was a sentence he'd read more times than he could count. He'd allowed the words to become him far more often than he'd ever admit. He'd kept it with him as a remembrance of the expectations he had to overcome in his own life. This time, however, when he unfolded the piece of paper and gazed at the writing pinched between his thumb and index finger, his throat closed up tight and his chest strained with pain.

He recognized the letters.

It was the same hand that scribbled the cursive words into the journal. He couldn't believe it. He couldn't bring himself to believe the journal held any significance in his life, much less the answers to why he was the way he was. Pages of the journal flipped back and forth with a speed he'd not dare exact before the idea in his head turned sour. The word *coward* repeated in his head over and over again, in the voice of his father, as he thumbed through the journal, forgetting to read anything as his swirling thoughts threatened to drown him right then and there. It lasted only seconds before he landed on a page that made his jaw fall open and his pupils dilate.

He memorized every swoop, swirl, and dot of the cursive writing to ensure he wasn't just imagining things, but the longer he examined that page in his palm and that piece of paper in his fingers, he realized there wasn't any amount of staring that would prove his worst suspicions wrong. Handwriting aligned with the words on the journal, the frayed edges of the paper were identical, stained yellow parchment pages bore no discernible differences from the note, and even the musty odor struck him as oddly similar.

There was chattering surrounding him, a buzzing of bugs against porch lights, a clattering of drink glasses, boots stomping on the floor, cigarette smoke filling the air, and the plucking of a lone acoustic guitar from a corner he couldn't recognize, but he couldn't pay attention to anything other than the words he couldn't look away from. They were becoming him. Every letter and space defined his very existence, no matter how hard he fought against it.

The page was torn midway through, with a chunk missing entirely, making up a section separated by what remained of the top and bottom of the parchment.

By my grandson's grandson, the name Robert Ford will be known all around this miserable world.

Rob didn't need to read the words again. He knew what it said. He knew all the way down to his bones what it said. He'd rehearsed the line over and over in his head, doing his best to forget the words despite being burned into his very soul. There was only one thing he'd been able to come to terms with since first laying his eyes on the piece of paper given to him by his father—the world certainly is miserable.

"Those will be the last son of a bitchin' words you ever say to me, you hear me?"

Rob had succumbed to the most far-fetched conspiracies he'd ever been able to conjure up in his mind. The cursive writing took on a different meaning, it became a different language, and even stranger, he could understand it like it was his own native tongue.

"You might as well apologize, it ain't no use in dying over nothing."

"You apologize, asshole!"

"You got here usin' those fancy, meaningless, fuckin' words, but I can guarantee you this, they won't save you now."

Rob allowed his thoughts to connect dots that had never been connected before. The mere possibility of the page he'd carried around for so long having come from the journal in his hands spurred his train of thought to what else could be true.

"I swear to God, I'll gut you. You will bleed out right here before anyone can touch you."

"You think you can close the distance faster than a forty-five bullet? I already got your name all over it."

"You better not miss, you mother fu—"

"Ain't no one else dying over this!"

Rob thought of his failures, of how the last few weeks had brought him no closer to freedom from his own actions, only further bound to their consequences. More than anything, however, he thought of Horse. No creature deserved such a fate, much less the only horse that could withstand his own sabotage. It was a moment in his life he would have never chosen to define him, but he knew it would nonetheless. He wished above anything else he'd been there to share its final moments in this miserable world.

That wish would come to change everything about his unfortunate circumstances. It set off a flurry of dominoing possibilities he couldn't bring himself to believe.

"No, dammit! There ain't no need to do all that."

"He's gonna die for that! You hear me? You're gonna fuckin' die for that!"

"It ain't that big of a deal. Just let it go, man."

"You hear him? He thinks he can talk his way out of a bullet."

"Not this time."

Bam.

"What the—" Rob turned around, snapping out of

his own rambling thoughts to the explosion of a gunshot blasting out in the confined walls of a camper parked out in the middle of nowhere.

He saw a twisted mixture of laughter and death at the front door. O'Kelley and Sam, drunk as the night is long, were standing over the body of a man he did not recognize. The dead man was not faceless, he surely had a name and a life he likely wanted to keep on living, but to Rob in that moment, the shot that took his life was a lightbulb. It was a figurative flip of a switch.

He watched the words on the journal come to life in front of his eyes, and he knew in his gut what was happening. He may never admit it to anyone aloud, he may never even admit it to himself, but he knew the journal was more than some scratch pad of the man who came to be known as *the coward Robert Ford*, the man who shot the outlaw Jesse James in the back of the head—it was his life playing out before his eyes.

"You gunned him down," Rob said, before thinking. "Why?"

"Didn't you hear him? The guy was threatening to turn us in, said he watched us haul ass out of the Coleman's family pasture," said O'Kelley.

"I tried to stop it," Sam chimed in. "I really did."

"You want to spend the rest of your life in some shithole jail?"

"I damn sure don't want to kill everyone who shows their face around us. Hicks wouldn't have wanted that either."

"Hicks didn't have a clue what the hell he wanted."

"Maybe I outta do the same thing to you, see how you like it," Sam shot back.

"Easy, y'all. Let's just catch our breath. That whole

thing went to shit back there, we lost some good people, and we're pretty much screwed six ways to Sunday. Nothing we can do about any of that. We need to lay low until we know what the hell is gonna happen to us. The last thing I want to do is make another call to the Bossman about how we went and made matters worse."

"I know."

"Yes, sir."

Rob was trembling. He was pulled back to his reading as soon as he was done lecturing the few men left standing. His fingers twitched, and his eyes darted back and forth as he walked through the eight-foot-wide camper. It was like he was craving a hit he'd never had before. He fumbled his way back to the journal, desperate to feast his eyes on words he could live by, unable to escape the loop of memories playing over and over in his head.

He flipped over the death of his horse, quickly finding the entry he'd last read, the one that told of the cost of loyalty before it was made real. He scanned the letters in awe, his mouth agape, his fingers struggling to grasp the corners of the page delicately enough to turn without creasing. His face was pressed closer to the page than he'd ever found himself before. Whiffs of leather and ink, soured with age, escaped the cracks and folds of the journal.

Rob couldn't help but notice it weighed heavier than he'd remembered. He allowed his imagination to stretch reality a little further. If the entries of the long-dead Robert Ford truly could put words to his own fate so many decades later, he couldn't help but consider what it could mean about what was in store for him.

He moved his hand to flip the page before he was

damn near knocked over by the impact of common sense finding its way back to his conspiracy-riddled brain.

"Get it together," he whispered.

The mere notion of the journal stolen from a random house by a dead man turning out to be the real Robert Ford, of being the same journal from which his dad's devious note, haunting his every move, was torn from, was more than he could believe. It was silly, really. The fact that his head could even come up with something so outlandish astounded him. Yet, even so, it was there nonetheless.

There was an urge inside him to read the entire journal, to know the twists and turns of the path in his own life. He fought the need with everything in him to turn the page even just once. He didn't know the rules of the words, or if there even were any, and he damn sure didn't want to ruin what could be found. As much as he wanted to, he knew it could only be a single entry at a time until he knew for sure. Ultimately, there was only one thing he could do, but he couldn't tell a single soul about it. It was an idea as far-fetched as the potential in the pages of the journal.

He'd have to test it for himself.

Against a backdrop of bickering between Sam and O'Kelley on what should be done about the dead body lying at the entrance of the camper, Rob allowed his eyes to feast on the words of the next entry in Robert Ford's journal.

July 5, 1881

It was just last night when everything went to hell, but it seems a lifetime ago. Today we were not burglars or murderers, nor trespassers or wrongdoers. We were cowboys. My prayers were answered in sweat and blood and dust. I was at long last able to forget about what my life had become or what may become of it. My dream of my name known around the world went away. My nightmares of death remained at bay. We heard about a bunch of horses following the river south. There wasn't much wrong with ours, but the price on the head of a good colt were more than we wanted to pass up on. It was worth our weight in gold to bring back half of those horses. We didn't do near as well as we'd hoped, but we did good enough. Boss says we're set for months. My brother is ready to get back on the trail now, though. He has always been greedy. He was cut out for this life. I was cut out for more. On the back of a two-year-old wilder than even the boss himself, I could feel the pull of freedom. It called my name. I almost felt a pain in my stomach when I saw the colt's eyes when it failed to throw me. It was breaking, same as me. Maybe that's just what it meant to be alive. Loss becomes us all in some kind of way. It doesn't care about what we want, it just is. For the unlucky horse who caught my rope around its neck, another victim felt its dreadful weight. Whether I did it for my own sake or the horse's, I didn't let the world have its way. I intervened. Despite the call of riches ringing in our ears as we rode into town with a couple dozen broken horses and the duty we were sworn to with one another keeping us together, I had thoughts of something else. I would never tell the boss, or even my brother, but that horse is tied up out back. It deserves a chance at freedom once again, and I do too. Who knows, maybe we will find it together.

Bob.

"He's gonna get us all killed, you know," Sam's

voice punctuated the end of the journal entry he was reading.

Rob had no choice but to turn his head and acknowledge the man who'd followed him into the unknown, to face down a wall of bullets. He deserved that much at least, despite how much Rob wanted only to focus on the little black book clutched in his fingers. "Who is?" he finally said.

"Who do you think I mean? The guy who's just shootin' anyone for lookin' at him wrong? That ain't how we've ever done things, and you don't seem to care. I'm tellin' you, I care."

"I do too, Sam," said Rob. "There's only three of us left now, though. Until Bossman gets us some new hands, we have to deal with who we've got. That's our job."

"It's our punishment. We're not here because it's what we wanted to be ever since we were growing up. We're here because we didn't turn out anything like what we were supposed to. We're fuckups. But even we deserve better than what that man will bring on us."

"I hear you."

"I don't think you do, Rob. I've known you long enough to know you don't wanna deal with the hard stuff, but you can't run from this one. As soon as you turn your back on him to start runnin', he'll put a bullet in your back."

"He ain't killin' any of us. Bossman would show him there are things worse than death, and he knows it."

"You think he cares about what's coming his way?"

Rob turned to see O'Kelley dragging the dead body away from the camper with both of his hands grasped around the arm of the one unfortunate enough to find himself on the other end of O'Kelley's gun. He'd bled out over the steps leading into the camper, and his boots made drag marks in the mud leading away from them. The man's cell phone was still lying in the dirt, and it started to vibrate as he was hauled away. Someone was looking for a man they'd never talk to again. Neither evidence nor false notions of right and wrong played a role in what O'Kelley was doing.

Sam was trying to tell him the only other hand left alive was careless and violent. Rob knew ambition when he saw it, though, and O'Kelley was ripe with it. The only thing that frightened him was the simple fact that O'Kelley believed himself to be untouchable.

"I'll keep an eye on him," said Rob.

"You better do more than that," answered Sam, as he tugged up on his button-down shirt to reveal a pocket .380 jammed into his waistband. With his thumb, he flicked the safety off before nodding at Rob. "Don't go to sleep without it. That's when people like him get the bravest."

"I'll try to remember that."

"We ain't gonna last much longer if all this keeps up," said Sam.

"We ain't gonna need much longer," Rob answered. "I got somethin' up my sleeve."

Chapter 13

There are few relationships important to a man in this world.

His mother, the first person he ever cared about, is among them. His wife, if he's lucky enough to find one, is more often than not the second person he allows himself to think about. When his life's on the line and the final stars he may ever see are shining down on him in the night sky, he will think of the miles he traveled and how it brought him to his final breath. These sparing moments of peace in his life will be shared with not his mother, nor his wife, they will be those shared with the horse that carried him along his lonesome path.

Rob was no different than any other man who called himself a cowboy. His sweat-stained hat on his head, the denim wrapped around his bent knees, and the leather reins in his calloused grip meant nothing without a horse to take him down the trail to see what was around the next bend. He was a man without a horse since that damn snake found its way inside, and that made him a man without much of a direction.

If the stolen journal could do what Rob suspected, what he so desperately needed for it to do, he would find himself a new horse tonight. That would be all the proof he'd need to know his life would be changed forever. Although he was too anxious to admit it even to himself, he knew it could also lead to the one thing he'd wanted to do ever since he got mixed up rustling cattle for the Bossman—run.

He was alone beneath the bright Texas stars overhead. Sam and O'Kelley were left behind to argue out their differences away from earshot of anyone who could make their situation worse. Rob wanted nothing to do with their feud, not when something as magnificent as the journal could still prove to be true. His boots mushed wet mud beneath every step as he ventured out into the woods without a destination, waiting to see what he would happen across. In one hand, he grasped a sixty-foot four-strand rope that had seen much better days in its time. Even so, he was familiar with the lasso when swinging above his head, and he trusted its movement to land where he needed when it mattered most. In the other hand, he grasped a fifty-pound leather saddle by the horn, slung over his shoulder to help support the weight.

There was a wall of pines, oaks, briar, yaupon, and every manner of dead timber fallen over in his path, each one home to screeching cicadas that made it difficult to think. Rob pushed on in the dark regardless. There was no flashlight to guide his steps, only what the moon could afford to spare him beneath the branches twisting in the sky, doing their best to blot out any hope for comfort.

Rob didn't need anything, though. He clutched the rope in his hands a little tighter and kept walking. If the journal was to be worthwhile, he'd be returning to the camper with his ass in the saddle strapped on the back of a new horse.

His arms burned from lactate buildup, his fingers felt like they would give way any minute, but he continued on. He was holding onto more than a rope and a saddle, he was holding onto hope for a chance at turning the tide in his favor for once in his forsaken life. People would call him crazy for doing what he was doing. Even he gave some thought to the fact that he should probably be in a white jacket for thinking the way he did. But he was willing to try anything. His dad did more than just deem him a coward from the day of his birth, there had to be more to it, there just had to be.

Before he knew it, the woods had dispersed behind him, and he walked out into an open pasture bordered on one side by a farm road with only an occasional car speeding by. It was fenced with decades-old wire and rotting posts, but it was enough to keep a docile herd in its place if needed. He trudged along, wishing he had a spare hand to wipe the sweat from his brow. There were bottom areas still holding water, daring him to soak his boots a little too high, and invisible holes dug by moles and armadillos, promising a broken ankle with every step. More troublesome than any of it, however, was the increasingly heavy journal tugging down his back pocket. It was the weight of the world he felt back there, plain and simple.

The night dragged on, only getting darker as silhouettes of clouds rolled into the sky to block the stars and moon from sight. The only signs of life were insects scrambling from his path and buzzing in the tree lines surrounding him. Rob knew all he had to go back to was more running from the very death that had already found the small outfit's trust in one another. It pushed him forward to find something else.

He'd gone into patches of trees and stretches of pastures, wandering aimlessly, waiting for something to happen. It went on for hours. The unified voice of nightfall from the cicadas and grasshoppers and warblers grew hoarse but never came to a stop. It was a constant, and he wanted with everything in him to allow it to become the soundtrack of his escape. Only pain came with such hope, and Rob found himself throwing something as foolish as hope into the journal rather than his own dreams.

Whether or not such intentions would pay off had yet to be seen. Rob walked on. He put one boot in front of the other, thoughtlessly in every sense of the word. Thoughts of Horse swirled in his head as he suppressed the questions arising from the journal. Did he cause the poor horse's death by reading the journal? If he did, maybe that meant he was to blame for Hicks' death and Cliff's, too. What else would he be responsible for? It was impossible to know for sure, but the only proof Rob needed tonight would be his ride back to the camper.

He'd lost track of time before he saw so much as a shadow move in the distance. There was no herd of horses rushing through the pines ready for Rob to take his pick. Most likely, it was a couple of hogs trying to tear up some old man's pasture looking for something to eat. He pressed on still.

The silhouette returned from the other side of the tree line, a pasture away. Rob was straddling a four-string barbed wire fence when he caught it out of the corner of his eye. Sharp ends jabbed into his thigh, promising to tear his jeans. His hands shook on the top strand as he tried to balance himself. It was trespassing, most likely, but he'd already thrown his saddle over the fence, so climbing over to retrieve it was happening one way or another. By the time he'd made it across and bent down to sling the saddle across his back, the silhouette made itself known once again.

"I'll be a son of a…" Rob whispered.

There it was, clear as the day hidden behind the other side of the world, standing at the other end of a twenty-acre pasture was the silhouette of a horse at least four years old. As soon as Rob's eyes had tracked it down in the darkness, it was gone. Before he could realize it, Rob was running through the pasture as eagerness overcame him. The weight of the saddle was closer to a feather now. The rope trailed behind him, lost to the whims of gravity as it whipped back and forth.

His frantic pace was interrupted by a scream that pierced through the cold night air, filling Rob's lungs. It was low and rumbling, and nothing that a horse could ever be responsible for. There was someone out there, not too far from where he stood. That meant the horse wasn't alone. It meant he'd stumbled into something he didn't fully understand. That was never of much consequence for men like Rob, though. He'd spent most of his life fumbling into just about every situation, and this would be no different. He clutched the saddle and rope in his hands a little tighter, took a deep breath, and ran after the horse's direction, completely ignoring what, or who, could still be out in the woods.

Whatever happened next, for the time he was out in the middle of some unknown guy's pasture, Rob cared only about the horse he knew had to be meant for him. It was the kind of feeling that would put your stomach in your throat, carrying your heart with it on the way, and it made Rob start to tremble as a result.

"You get back here, you stupid piece of shit! You hear me?"

The man's voice boomed from the trees no more than fifty yards in front of Rob. He was either in the wrong place at the wrong time, or that man was. Rob had a feeling deep down in his belly that he was exactly where he was supposed to be. Instead of turning to whip out his pistol and stick himself in yet another fight he wasn't prepared for, he held tight to the saddle and rope and took off again after the horse.

"I'm gonna fuckin' kill you!" The man's voice came through again. "You won't throw another goddamn man from your back ever again! I'm puttin' a bullet in your head as soon as I find you!"

Rob was listening as he ran, but none of the words meant anything to him. The only thing that really meant anything was the possibility that he could be riding a horse back to the camper any minute and that every word in the journal would then be proven as unequivocally true. It was all too good to believe, but he had to catch the fleeing horse first. Until then, everything was a fantasy in his head. Without the horse, he was just another insane criminal making up realities that were never there, and he belonged locked away from society.

Boom.

Rob ducked low and stumbled into the dirt at the blasting of a rifle from just behind him. There was no way to know for sure if the rifle had been aimed in his direction, but he had no intention of sticking around long enough to find out. He started sprinting. Putting distance between him and whoever was firing into the night behind him as fast as he could.

He was racing as fast as his legs would carry him, holding just about everything he owned in his hands, when it hit him. He was doing exactly what he wanted most—running. To Sam and O'Kelley, he'd packed his shit and hauled ass into the night, literally sprinting in the opposite direction yet again.

As the minutes ticked by, he couldn't help but question his own sanity. Had he made this whole thing up to justify doing the one thing he knew he had no real shot at actually doing? It was a potential he couldn't ignore, and even started to give some real consideration, before the high-pitched cry of a neighing horse echoed in the trees all around him. It came from every direction. The panicked bawling of a horse that would disorient and rattle men who'd seen less only served to strengthen Rob's resolve. It was the exact kind of reassurance he needed to know it wasn't his own mind playing tricks on him.

There was a horse out there. It was up to Rob to track him down, rope him, and get his saddle strapped over his back. He ran without fearing any consequences of what it looked like. He ran with a saddle and rope toward a horse that would change his life from this night forward. He ran toward a fate controlled by something other than the most demeaning words his own father could find about him.

Boom.

Another shot only pushed Rob to run a little faster into the night. He knew there was no way he could catch up to a horse running away from him, not unless the horse wanted to be caught. He continued on anyway.

"I know where you're goin'! Coyotes will be eatin' good tonight!"

Rob paid no attention to the man's insults and threats. He just kept running. He'd been running so long he didn't even remember how long he'd been out of breath for. Adrenaline coursed through him, but his burning muscles and lungs could not be soothed. He kept running, though. Heavy, muddy boots stomped against the earth as he plowed forward with only one thing on his mind.

He was right.

The silhouette of a horse appeared in the distance again, further than it should've been at any natural pace, but there nonetheless. It was a phantom in the night, a ghost disappearing behind the trees. It was a spectral presence before it was ever mane and muscle and hoof. There were few sights Rob would ever hope to see more in his life, and this one made him damn near double an already exhaustive pace.

"Get back here, you motherfucker!"

The man's voice bellowed throughout the trees. This time, his threats were backed up by the clanking of a bolt from a rifle jamming in a new cartridge. He was closer than Rob had thought. The saddle felt like it weighed two hundred pounds now. The rope had unraveled almost completely and dragged behind him. It was all a burden. For the first time, Rob considered himself lucky to have the six-shooter still strapped to his hip. Whoever was chasing that horse down didn't seem to be all that happy about what was going on.

Rob pushed through a patch of brush with his

shoulder. Briar thorns slapped against his face as he shoved through to the other side. He kept moving without thinking of where he was. By the time he looked around, he found himself in a circular clearing lined with towering pines with an American Paint standing seventeen hands tall staring right at him.

The saddle finally fell from Rob's hands, slamming into the dirt with a noticeable *thud*. He stood still for a few seconds, monitoring the horse's demeanor and testing what might set it off. His heart pounded in his chest from the sprint, and the blood was still trying to find its way back into his fingers. His wildest suspicions were made real before his eyes, and the only thing he had to do now was finish the job.

His first step toward the horse was met without so much as a slight reaction. It encouraged him to take another, then another. The horse's gaze was locked on him, and nothing he did dared break it. Rob held his breath for what felt like ten minutes, until his chest was about to explode. When he was standing side by side with the paint, he exhaled at last, and the horse finally moved. It tilted its massive head and turned to nudge Rob on the shoulder, as if urging him to continue.

The worn rope slid over the horse's neck with ease, and before Rob knew what was happening, they were walking side by side back to his saddle at the tree line as the man's threats continued to ring out in the trees around him. A surreal wave of disbelief washed over Rob, and he forgot about his burning muscles and short breath in an instant.

Rob's old saddle and blanket rested perfectly on the Paint's back, and the strap wrapped beneath it to slide into the D-ring almost as if it was a custom-built rig for that singular horse. He'd never experienced anything like it before. Rob tugged on the straps and secured both the front and rear rigging before he reached up to gently pat the horse on the neck a couple of times. His affection was matched when the horse flapped its lips softly. Rob took advantage of the reaction by gently inserting the mouthpiece of the bit into its mouth, adjusting the shanks and looping the reins just where he always liked them.

When the saddle was set, the American Paint seemed to know what came next. Rob positioned himself beside the stirrup and watched as the horse lowered its head and tightened its spine, preparing for Rob's ascent. When he planted his ass in the saddle, everything had become right in the world, and Rob could see a lifetime ahead. One where he wasn't in debt to the worst men he'd ever known. One where he had paid his debt to society and held his freedom, too. Hell, even a life where he could chase something that made him happy instead of something that only kept him out of handcuffs.

"I see you, you son of a bitch! You better get the hell off my horse, he's mine to shoot if I want!"

Rob's heels nudged the sides of the Paint, and off they went. Hooves glided across the dirt like it was ice, and the wind brushed drops of sweat from Rob's forehead as they ran. They hadn't been moving for more than five seconds before a rifle opened fire from somewhere behind them.

Boom.

A bullet whistled by Rob and lodged into a tree, sending splinters flying into the air in

every direction. Rob ducked his head, but the horse pushed harder. They were too far away to hear the rifle chamber another round, but they were close enough to still come under fire.

Boom.

Another bullet just barely missed them, slamming into the earth and sending dirt spewing into the air just fifteen feet in front of their path.

The horse never faltered. It ran like it was the only thing it knew how to do in life. This time, there were no bullets that followed and no fury-filled threats crying out into the night. It was only the rush of the wind and the rhythm of hooves hitting the pasture that filled Rob's ears, and it was the sweetest music he'd ever heard in his life. He was serenaded in the notes of his own escape, and he never wanted it to end.

A part of Rob wanted to keep running, to push the horse further and further until they were in another state, or even another country. He wanted to ride this moment as far as it would take him. He knew that wasn't an option, but he sure wished for it anyway. The horse he'd stolen seemed to want the same thing as him. No matter how hard he tugged against the reins or directed the horse to ease up, it pushed on harder and harder. A hard bounce in the saddle soon evened out as the horse found its stride in the open field. Rob bent his knees a little more and leaned forward, accepting whatever fate would have in store this time. They were at a dead sprint, and he allowed himself a few seconds to dream about it never coming to an end.

The horse may have been running toward freedom, but Rob was running back into servitude. He was indebted by his own actions, and the consequences would follow him wherever he went. After he threw all his eggs in the same basket of violence and lawlessness, the only way to get them back was to match them at their own game. Until he did that, death would wait behind every door and lurk just around every corner.

The American Paint finally began to slow its pace to a more manageable trot. Rob knew what was happening, and he patted the journal still stowed in his back pocket. He had a lot to thank it for, and now there wasn't much left to do except read the next entry and prepare for the next step in his path to achieving the same feeling the horse beneath him was experiencing. He took a deep breath, filling his lungs with the cool air of the night, and looked around to make sure no one was within eyesight. Then, he started to sing.

> *And they rode together through the hills and*
> *plains,*
> *And they rode together through the sun and*
> *rain.*
> *They were a team, a cowboy and his horse,*
> *And they were a team of the wild and free.*

Chapter 14

Why does evil always have a way of rearing its ugly face?

Rob was a man born to be on the run, that much he had come to accept. He was not a man capable of great evil, or at least that's what he liked to think about himself. Robbie Ford, the cattle rustler, was a lowly thief obligated by debt, yet driven by freedom. He was not inclined to inflict pain and suffering, he only wanted to get by, but the world, for one reason or another, always had other ideas.

When Rob returned to the camper riding his newest partner in the outfit, a brilliant American Paint stallion in his prime, he didn't find two men waiting for his leadership and direction to change the night for the better. They were both standing across from one another, staring each other down like their lives depended on it. It was an awkward situation to barge into, especially at a time when Rob only wanted to show off his new horse and apply the lessons of the next journal entry to save them all from sharing a fate similar to Hicks and Cliff.

"That man is a damn rat, Rob!" Sam hollered before waiting on anything else to happen.

"That's exactly what a no-good fuckin' rat would say," O'Kelley answered.

Rob sighed.

At first, Rob thought they were just about to fight one another. As he came closer, still sitting in the saddle, he realized they were both with their hands over their hips. He'd walked into a shootout waiting to happen. They stood beneath the white LEDs zip-tied to the top of the camper, casting an unnatural glow on their feud. Sam was in faded jeans and an open flannel with a stained white tank beneath, his fade was over-grown, and a silver necklace peeking from behind the warped and wrinkled collar. O'Kelley kept his cowboy hat low and his t-shirt tucked behind the grip of a polymer 9mm pistol jammed into his waistband haphazardly.

"The hell are y'all two bickerin' about now?"

"Someone told the Colemans we'd be there and got Hicks and Cliff shot dead," said Sam. "There was only a handful of people who knew what was goin' on, and they're all standing right here.

"How do you know someone ratted us out?"

"Don't be stupid," O'Kelley butted in. "Of course, someone said something. They were waiting on us. Didn't even have to load their rifle, they just started shootin'."

"Even if someone did," Rob tried to reason his way through the latest scuffle. "What would they have to gain from getting all of us killed?"

"Aside from the money they got from selling us out?" Sam asked a rather valuable question.

"Hmm," said Rob, who was starting to buy into a conspiracy he'd only just learned about seconds prior. "You have a point. Shit did go south a lot quicker than it ever has for us. Even if that wasn't our first time getting shot at, we usually have to at least make a mistake before someone opens fire. This time, we barely made it onto the property."

"It couldn't have been Hicks or Cliff, either," said O'Kelley. "Why would they do something to get themselves killed?"

"Well, in their defense, neither of them were the sharpest tool in the old shed," Rob lamented.

"I ain't buyin' that coincidence," said Sam. "That man right there has been screwing us ever since he joined up. I'm telling you, ain't nothing gone right with him privy to information he don't need to know nothing about."

"What the hell do you know? I've been doing this longer than both of y'all dipshits combined. You want to talk about screwing us up? How about we talk about the wall of bullets Rob here just walked us right into."

"You really are an asshole, aren't you, O'Kelley?"

"He's deflecting," said Sam. "He don't want us connecting the dots."

"You can connect all you want, but you lift that hand up of yours and you won't ever connect anything ever again. I'll shoot you both dead right here, and I won't think twice about it."

"Sure sounds innocent, don't he?"

"I got nothing to hide," O'Kelley started to make his case. "I'm here for the same reason you are. I killed a man I shouldn't have, and I got caught with blood on my hands. Bossman was the only one who could wash it off before the government found me, just like he did for both of you. I ain't stupid. But we all know his help comes at a cost, and it's one no one could ever hope to afford."

Rob nudged the horse closer to stand across from both Sam and O'Kelley. All he could think about now was how to defuse the escalating situation. There wasn't much that could be said. Those two were about as hard-headed as it gets. If they were gonna duke it out, it was gonna happen one way or another. He needed both of them alive if he was going to pull off whatever was in that journal.

With a flick of his wrist, Rob yanked the revolver from its cracked leather holster resting at his side. He aimed it at O'Kelley first, then at Sam.

"Here's what we're gonna do," he said, still bouncing the end of his barrel back and forth. "First, you're both gonna take those pistols you keep thinking about drawing, and you're gonna toss them on the ground right over here beside me."

Sam didn't move. Neither did O'Kelley. Their hands hovered above their hip, still as a pond in August. Both were refusing to be the first to obey what their more immediate boss was telling them.

Rob's calloused thumb gently pressed the hammer back until it clicked into place.

O'Kelley was the first to submit. He sighed and grabbed his pistol, then threw it in the dirt right beside the hooves of Rob's new horse. Sam hesitated for only a few more seconds before he did the same. The stallion huffed when the second pistol slid into the ground, but didn't flinch.

"That's better," Rob said. "Freeing, ain't it? Now,

we need to get back to business, but I ain't gonna close my eyes around y'all until I know the bullets ain't gonna start flying as soon as I fall asleep. So, unless y'all got any other ideas, you're gonna ball up that fist of yours and you're gonna get to swinging at one another until you don't have the breath to keep doin' it."

This time, Sam had no hesitation in him. His right fist landed against O'Kelley's jaw with a crack that made Rob wonder whether it was O'Kelley's face or Sam's knuckle that just broke. Either way, both of the men collided in a flurry of fists with gnashing teeth and scrambling feet. They were fighting not just to hurt one another, but to take a life. Rob knew it was going to be bad, but it was necessary if he hoped to keep them both alive.

O'Kelley took a step back from getting his nose bashed in and attempted to recollect himself. His face was beet-red, and his chest huffed with every breath. His eyes were locked on Sam, hoping to find a way around his incoming blows, but somehow reacting too slowly, catching every one of them right where Sam had intended it to land. A stream of crimson split in two above his upper lip and trailed down the sides of his face.

Sam saw blood and went for more. He rained down one punch after another, ignoring anything coming his direction. Before he realized it, O'Kelley had ripped his chain from his neck, scratched his cheek deep enough to draw his own blood, and swung a boot right into his groin.

Rob watched the scuffle with disappointment sinking into his belly. Dust rose into the air, turning into a cloud surrounding the two like a cage they couldn't escape until only one remained who could draw breath into his lungs. Sam may have been winning the fight, but O'Kelley didn't back down for nothing. The new guy would take a few steps back every so often to get his bearings, then charge right back into the fray. Sam seemed to never run out of energy. His swings never slowed down, nor lost their impact. Every strike sounded like a bone cracking in half.

The circle Sam and O'Kelley were beating each other half to death inside was soon more blood than dirt. It's metallic tinge rose into Rob's nostrils. Sam finally landed his right hook into O'Kelley's left eye socket, and things went downhill from there. When the new guy's back hit the earth, Sam was on top of him in an instant, dropping one blood-covered fist after another onto an already bruised and battered face.

"Shit!" O'Kelley yelped.

Rob kept his ass planted in the saddle, looking down at the fight.

"You gonna help? He's about to kill me!"

"Shut...the...hell...up!"

Every punch sounded like a crack of lightning ringing out across the sky. O'Kelley held his arms up as best he could and squirmed beneath Sam's knees, squeezing into his ribs. It did no good, though. He eventually lost the strength to protect himself, and that's when the most damage was dealt. Sam didn't let up. O'Kelley was either playing possum or was actually unconscious. Judging from the impact and spurts of blood from each of Sam's strikes, Rob was starting to believe he wasn't faking much.

After a couple minutes longer than he should have waited, Rob finally nudged his horse forward. The Paint knew exactly what Rob was hoping to achieve. It took a few silent steps forward, then used its long head to pry Sam off of O'Kelley, propping him back up on his feet with an effortless toss. Rob eased the reins back and stopped when he could make eye contact with Sam.

"You kill him?"

"Not yet."

"What did I miss?"

"His phone rang when he wasn't expecting it. When he looked at me to see if I'd noticed, I saw everything I needed to see in his eyes. I should've killed him right then and avoided this whole mess."

"So, you don't have proof? You just think he ratted us out and got half our outfit killed on a hunch?"

"I don't need any proof," said Sam. "I know what I saw."

"You want me to gun down that man based on a look? Do you even hear yourself? Son of a bitch, Sam. This ain't easy as it is, I don't see why in Sam Hill you gotta make it even harder for no damn good reason."

"Go on then, shoot me dead and get it over with."

"Now I know you aren't listening, you stubborn jackass," Rob scolded him.

O'Kelley grunted in his forced nap, blood still running from his nose, mixing with sweat and snot, before pooling on the ground beneath his head. It was a sad sight, and maybe one he deserved, but Rob didn't know for sure, and because of that, he couldn't let it continue.

"I told you, I was onto something. You need to cut

the shit and let me get us out of this mess," he continued. "We can't do it by ourselves, though. As soon as Bossman finds out you and I are the last ones alive, he's gonna cut his losses and kill us both. If there's three of us, maybe he's more inclined to just send more bodies to throw at the problem. I don't know about you, but I know which one I'd prefer."

"The one that keeps me alive."

"Exactly."

"So, what are we supposed to do with him?"

"You just pull yourself together. This whole thing is over. Y'all fought it out, it's time to drop it."

"I'm telling you, if we trust him much longer, he's gonna get us killed just like he did to Hicks and Cliff. You're making a mistake letting him live."

"Let me deal with him," said Rob, kneeling down to check the pulse of O'Kelley, just to make sure he was still ticking. When he was satisfied with what he felt, he stood back up and stared through Sam. "Drag him into the camper, don't say another word until we can all sit down and talk."

IT WOULD BE three hours before Rob, Sam, and an only half-conscious O'Kelley were staring at each other across from a tiny table inside the camper. The air conditioning struggled to run, failing entirely to cool the camper to any comfortable temperature. For Rob and Sam, the heat only caused a few beads of sweat to trail down their forehead. For O'Kelley, however, his face was on fire with swelling and blood still drying to his lips and nose. The sweltering feeling of the camper only added to the tension that could be sliced with the blunt side of a butter knife.

Rob watched as the two men refused to acknowledge one another. In this line of business, dealing with violent souls was just another day. The trick to managing them was to give them something else to fight rather than each other. That was exactly what Rob was going to do.

"Doesn't matter if someone sitting at this table is a rat. We're all gonna die if we keep going down this road," Rob explained. "I've been doing this long enough to know that's what happens to people like us. We get killed so crooks and criminals can keep draggin' down the rest of the world and collecting paychecks for doin' it."

"What the hell does this have to do with us?" Sam shifted in his seat as he spoke.

"It means we're gonna do something about it."

O'Kelley didn't say anything. Rob wasn't sure if he even could. His jaw was slack from the beating, and his lips were purple behind stained blood. His eyes were bloodshot, and only one could be opened all the way. Rob could smell the iron in the blood all over his face and clothes.

"We already know what we have to do. We pay our debt. That's how this whole thing works. We steal cattle for the Bossman to sell. We pay off our debt, and he lets us walk. We all signed the same contract."

"That's exactly right," said Rob. "We pay off our debt."

O'Kelley leaned in closer to the table.

"We've been sitting around waiting on Bossman to tell us what to do instead of taking initiative. I'm gonna change all that. We could end this whole damn nightmare in a few hours if we do this right."

"What you got in mind?"

"I'll explain, but first I gotta know that you two won't try to kill each other when I go to sleep. Is that too much to ask?"

Sam turned to O'Kelley at last. There was a pause before the man who'd been beaten half to death returned the look in Sam's direction. They held their gaze until a mutual agreement had formed, one that didn't need to be spoken, only understood.

This was enough for Rob. He smacked his palms down on the table harder than he'd ever intended, sending the particle board and laminate-wrapped table splintering to the ground in three separate pieces. He couldn't let them know what would be guiding them to their freedom. He didn't even know for himself, to be completely honest. But he was willing to trust whatever path the journal led them down—for better or worse.

"Time to get some sleep, boys," Rob said, and stood up, kicking the pieces of the table to the side and tilting up his cowboy hat. "Tomorrow, we're gonna take our freedom for ourselves."

Sam stared at Rob with distrust in his eyes. It was justified, all things considered, but the longer Rob stared back, the more he could see the distrust give way to loyalty. It was a loyalty Rob had earned through fire and blood.

O'Kelley had his own stare, and when Rob glanced over at him, he knew right then and there Sam was being truthful. Something inside O'Kelley was twisted, no matter how much he said otherwise. While he may have said the right things, and fought alongside them, there wasn't a single hint of loyalty in his eyes. Rob would have to be careful with whatever happened next, because not only was Sam right, but so was Cliff. It was his final words. He knew what was happening, and he tried to warn everyone. Rob may not have been able to do anything about it just yet, but he knew deep down what was happening.

There was a rat in what was left of their ranks.

Chapter 15

"You don't need to tell me what in the goddamn hell is goin' on in my county!"

"I'm saying you need help, Sheriff."

"I don't need a son of a bitchin' thing from you."

"How long until someone turns up dead?"

"If someone does turn up dead, that blood is on your hands. You hear me? I told a hundred different agencies a hundred different times about what was goin' on out here. I told y'all the cartel was here. I told y'all people were dying and God knows what else was going on because of what was goin' on. You know what I was told?"

"We don't need to go over this again."

"I was told to shut up and write more highway tickets."

"That is not what you were told, and you know that."

"Now you want to tell me we got a problem? Like I don't already fuckin' know it?"

"We approved every request for assistance you've

made. You are the one tryin' to play cowboy out there. That blood won't be on my hands, Sheriff. It'll be on yours and you know it."

"Is there anything else?"

"We've got a couple people coming your way to lend a hand. They'll be there in three days. You have that long to clean up whatever mess you've made."

The phone resting on the corner of Sheriff Turpin's desk went flying across the room until it smashed into the wall and broke into several pieces on the floor. Tom shook his hand in pain as the redness in his cheeks grew hot with anger. His chest was thumping harder than he wanted, forcing him to plop himself down in an old, squeaking office chair. At his age, blood pressure was something he should be thinking about more often, but he never did. This time, his eyes felt like they were going to pop right out of his skull.

His hands were trembling when he picked up the pieces of the phone off the floor. It wasn't the first time he'd lost his cool and destroyed the damn thing. With a few curses uttered beneath his breath, he assembled the broken bits as best he could and assembled the phone again. It wasn't half a second after he had plugged it back into the outlet beneath his desk that it started ringing once again.

Tom's blood pressure started to rise again. Every ring sent a chill down his spine. It took everything he had in him not to hurl the contraption against the wall yet again. Instead, he took a deep breath, exhaled softly, relaxed his shoulders, and lifted the receiver of the phone.

"Sheriff Turpin," he said.

Through the other end of the line, the voice of the

one man he wanted more than anyone else to never talk to him again, came through. It was soft, yet firm, and assured in a sense of self-righteousness no one should have when speaking to someone in Tom's position. It was Dalton D. Woodson and he wanted answers Tom didn't have.

"Why aren't they gone?"

"Dalton, I appreciate you calling to check in on our business together, but I need—"

"I'm sorry, are you telling me that *you* need something?"

"It's not like that."

"If you ask me, I'd say you need your head on your shoulders. Something you are becoming dangerously close to losing. Once that happens, there's no going back, you know?"

"I understand."

"We talked about this over and over again. You reassured me, those kids would be taken care of before my speech. Well, guess what, I'm about to announce my candidacy for Congress, and those mother fuckers are running home to their moms and dads and telling everyone who'll listen about where they were held at. Everything points to me."

"I know, sir, I am—"

"You aren't doing shit! It's too late now. I've got a few dozen more getting smuggled in tonight, and the last thing I need is some government agency knocking on my door, or worse, kicking it in. You exist to make sure that don't happen, you hear me?"

"They won't be doing—"

"Everything will go down the drain if that happens. Do you understand me, Tom? That means you, too. You will be the first one thrown behind bars

for the rest of your worthless, shitty life. I don't care
how you do it, but you better make sure not a single
one of those kids can be traced back to me."

"You don't want to be talking like this on this line,"
Tom finally got out. "This is my office. I don't know
who is listening."

"Is that a threat? Are you really fuckin' threatening
me right now?"

"No, sir, I just—"

"If I wanted, not a single soul would ever hear hide
nor hair from you again. With a snap of my fingers, I
could make you fall off the face of the earth, and no
amount of badges or taxpayer dollars would ever
change that."

"I know."

"If you don't want to end up stuffed into an oil
drum halfway across the world, I'd suggest you get it
fixed, before my big day. All you gotta do is say *yes sir*,
hang up the phone, and go clean up your goddamn
mess."

"Yes, sir," said Tom, before gently placing the
handset back onto the base to end the call.

Out of nowhere, a sudden burst of rage overtook
Sheriff Tom T. Turpin, and with a red, swollen face,
he grabbed the handset once again, lifted it high into
the air, and slammed it back down onto the base. He
did it again, and again, and again, harder every time,
before the plastic broke in half, and he was left
punching the remains of the phone into the desk.

"FUCK!" Tom screamed as he kept punching the
desk, gripping what was left of the handset in his right
hand.

His lungs were on fire. His chest heaved up and
down, and he could feel the blood coursing through his

extremities at a frantic rate. He knew his blood pressure was completely shot at this point, but he didn't care. Sweat beaded up on his forehead and trailed down his creased face, some landing in his eyes and others falling onto the desk he hovered over. His pearl snap had somehow come undone at the top two snaps, leaving his chest hanging out more than was professionally acceptable.

Once again, the outburst forced him to fall back into the squeaking chair tucked away behind his desk. He focused on catching his breath, the aging HVAC running continuously in the old building, even the ticking of his clock hung up on a nail on the other side of the room. He focused on anything other than his entire world falling apart before his eyes. Everything he worked for was at stake and he'd have to betray it all if he hoped to live long enough to see retirement.

When he wanted privacy the most, to not hear another human's voice creep its way into his ears, the office door with closed blinds began to slowly open. Tom watched the scratched, golden doorknob rotate before none other than Denise herself poked her head around the other side of the door. Her eyes were red and puffy, like she'd just watched her dog die, and her voice quivered when she spoke.

"Those children," she stammered. "Those children they found at the Colemans' place. They started talking. You're gonna want to hear it for yourself, Tom."

"Is it bad?"

Denise's sobs were all that he was faced with for asking such a question. The door slammed shut this time, and Tom listened as the woman scurried away to hide her tears and return to the always-upright assistant he knew her to be.

Tom's head hung low as he left his office. He was hit with reports from other officers, administrators rushing back and forth between desks, and sniffles from Denise, who had found her way back to her desk. A stapled packet of warm, freshly printed papers was shoved into his chest. He didn't have to move his eyes very far at all to see the words he never wanted to read make themselves real right in front of him.

The report had been written by an officer named James Stone, who just so happened to have been in the area when the Colemans called the sheriff's office to let them know about some missing children who turned up on their doorstep. Stone's report began with the obvious, but soon dived into details that were tough to stomach when just reading, and surely unimaginable to actually endure.

Tom scanned through the packet and pushed it back at the officer who handed it to him. He walked by the rows of individual rooms where each of the children were still being questioned, and to the surprise of just about everyone in the building, he kept walking right out the front door. Tom didn't stop until he was standing in front of the driver's side door of his trusted pickup. He yanked on the handle and tossed his straw hat on the dash before sliding behind the wheel and slamming the door shut behind him. Tears streaked down the stubble on his cheek, but he didn't bother to wipe them away. He tried not to think about them and reached for the keys to crank the old V6 motor once again. It idled quietly as the tears continued to flow. There was no use in trying to stop them, he was mourning the death of his lifetime of work. It was his own actions to blame, and it made him want to drive that ragged F150 right into a tree going eighty miles an hour without his seatbelt. That wasn't an option, though.

Years and years of working to no end to clean up the county hasn't just yielded no results, it's gotten worse. Addiction and gambling, thieving and killing, it's all gone rampant over the last decade, and Tom lacked the resources and staff to do much to stop the tide. It was an inevitable evil, that's what Mr. Woodson had told him when he promised to give him what he needed. There were more promises made than he could ever keep count of, and he was just jaded enough to sell out in the hopes of only a few coming to fruition. He had the best of intentions when he made his deal with the devil, but he was facing the consequences now.

His boot finally pushed down gently on the gas pedal, and Tom drove off. He wanted desperately for the F150 to keep accelerating until all of his troubles were left behind. Its motor would be his golden ticket to a life free from the mistakes, promising to become his downfall. It would take him to a beach somewhere, or maybe even the mountains, anywhere but the pines looking down on him and the pastures threatening to swallow him whole. Tom pressed a little harder on the gas pedal, and the truck hummed in response. He pushed a little harder, and the cabin found a new rattle from somewhere inside the dash.

The truck found seventy-five on the speedometer with relative ease. Trees turned to a green blur, and the white lines on the side of the road became his only guide. Tom squinted his eyes and gripped the leather steering wheel tight enough to creak beneath his fingers. Vibrations overtook the cabin as the speedometer reached closer to eighty miles an hour.

A few years ago, Sheriff Tom got a call at two in the morning about an eighteen-wheeler turned over in the middle of the highway, and an SUV wrapped around a tree not too far away in a ditch. It's the kind of call people in his line of work dread every single day, the one they think about every time they clock in, and the one they have nightmares about when they close their eyes.

It was almost a head-on collision, but the SUV swerved at the last minute. The eighteen-wheeler had no chance of getting out of the way in time. The rain didn't help. By the time Tom showed up, there wasn't much he could even do except see enough to scar him the rest of his life. It was before he'd given up on his ideals of justice and good triumphing over evil, he was holding on to those fragile dreams until there was nothing left to grasp.

What stuck out to him during that night the most was the fact that the SUV was doing eighty miles an hour on a highway running through town with a posted fifty-five speed limit. When he saw what was left of the family of four inside, some of his final hopes of right and wrong were destroyed in fire and blood.

When Tom saw his speedometer reach that all-too-familiar number, the gore of that night long ago flashed across his mind and his boot instinctively fell off the gas pedal. He didn't have it in him. By the time his pickup had reached a more reasonable speed, he was approaching the single lane backroad he'd actually set out for when he left the station.

There was a fifteen-minute drive down that beat-up, bumpy, barely-paved road that was touchy at best for the V6 Tom was driving. It was times like this he wished he'd sprung for the Four Wheel Drive. Just as he started to consider whether or not he'd turned down the wrong back road, an oversized steel warehouse appeared over the tree line in the distance.

Tom sighed as he pulled his truck up to what seemed like an abandoned building, overgrown with brush and briar, where there wasn't a single soul to be found in a twenty-mile radius—except for the two armed men who came rushing out of the warehouse looking as pissed off as a red wasp about to sting. He knew the drill. He threw the truck into park and lifted his hands to show the men approaching both sides of his vehicle. The driver's door flung open, and Tom was dragged onto the ground in an instant.

"Who told you to come out here?" The first man, bearded and already sweating, put his knee in Tom's back as he hollered at him. "No one told you to bring your fat ass out here, Sheriff!"

"You know better than to show up like this unannounced, Tom," the other bearded one said, only a few pounds skinnier than his partner.

"I couldn't call," Tom spoke into the dirt. "I didn't know who was listening."

"The hell does that mean?"

"It means there are more coming. It means those kids you let run out of here are talkin' real loud and they got plenty of people to listen."

"Call him," said the skinny one.

Tom felt the knee release off of his spine, and he finally took a deep breath. A chubby, calloused hand that matched his own reached out to pull him back to his feet. This time, Tom took a second to grab the straw cowboy hat from his desk and jam it down over his head before he followed the two men pushing sidearms back into the holsters on their hips into the warehouse.

Just inside those rusted, steel walls were the exact sights that horror movies were made of. It was a retail store for the cartel, stocked with the kinds of things international criminal networks would kill a hundred times over. Cages of men, women, and children, malnourished, and beaten, lined one of the walls. Stacks of every kind of drug imaginable were stacked on the other wall. There were rows of what were almost certainly illegal firearms with more ammunition than an army needed to invade the southern border, a walled-off area filled with professional stage lighting and cameras, and aisles of drones, laptops, television screens, radios, and things Tom couldn't even recognize, all mixed with every type of explosive and drug paraphernalia imaginable.

The sheriff should have been shocked, but it wasn't the first time he'd been in such a place. This was one of several warehouses stashed across East Texas and the largest one in his county. It was everything he'd ever let slip under his nose for Mr. Woodson's enterprise to thrive, all bundled up in the same building. They moved constantly, never in one place for too long, but Tom was always aware when they set up in his county.

Before he got more than a few steps inside the building, a half-naked woman with drowsy eyes and a sluggish stroll came walking by, casually putting a single finger on Tom's shoulder before leaving as quick as she'd come. The sheriff couldn't help but brush off his shoulder where he'd been touched before pushing forward into the warehouse.

It reeked of musk and gunpowder, set against

constant whiffs of sewage and gasoline. Tom's boots splashed against standing, brown water with every step, and he did everything he could to not think about what it really was. Unimaginable horrors were taking place inside more of these buildings than most law enforcement agencies would be willing to admit. They were epicenters of business for more than just crooks and criminals with a little extra cash stuffed into their pockets. They were distribution hubs for organized crime. Considering where they were located in Texas and the clientele most often associated with Mr. Woodson, it didn't take long for Tom to realize he'd gotten into bed with more than one cartel from down south.

These people weren't just in the business of drugs, or trafficking, or arms dealing. They were running a monopoly on all of it, and Mr. Woodson was their merchant. Tom was just another cog in a wheel of corruption and cowardice, allowing it to happen under the guise of necessary evil. Thoughts of his own failures were swirling in his head as he found himself in a place that manifested his worst fears about what was happening on his watch.

When he approached a graying man sitting at a metal desk with his face buried in a stack of papers, it was these thoughts that encouraged him to finally do something that wasn't about himself. The man looked up at Tom and squinted his eyes as if he couldn't make out who was standing in front of him, then panic overtook him, and he scrambled frantically behind the desk, eventually falling backward in his chair and slamming his head against the concrete slab.

When the man looked up at Tom, the sheriff said only three words, "Pack your shit."

Chapter 16

The sun's light at dawn streaked across the sky to spark one of the biggest ideas Rob has ever had in his life.

He was reading yet another entry in Robert Ford's journal, soaking in the yellowed pages and cursive swoops from a pen held by his namesake generations ago. He thumbed through the entries he'd already read, recounting just how many of the events detailed inside had come to pass in his own life. It was unnatural and made his stomach flip with each new sentence, but he couldn't put it down.

Those words had become something like a hit of nicotine to him. He craved them. There was some insatiable part of him that needed to study every page, to memorize what was written and what it meant. He couldn't pry his eyes from the journal even if he wanted to. His eyes scanned each line with desperate intent, all to the background of a humming diesel engine racing down the highway with no destination in mind.

With Sam in his usual driver's seat, O'Kelley took to the back to both figuratively and literally nurse his wounds. There was an unfamiliar voice in the cabin this time, though. Another body had been fed to the grinder from Bossman. The man's name was Bill Pitts, and he was about as quiet as a nervous mute in the middle of church service. There wasn't much to talk about, and most of the men who'd come to the outfit pretty much knew what was in store for them. Rob didn't bother to ask about his ambitions or even why he'd been given the unfortunate assignment to come work with them. Bill Pitts was in debt, just like the rest of them, and there was only one way out of it.

Rob stopped reading when he reached the entry that had led him to find his new horse, the American Paint, who was on the run from an owner hellbent on putting a bullet in the beast before he'd stepped in. Rob basked in the sheer weight of fate in his hands. He let it fill him with hope that one day, he would finally be able to run from everything he'd made for himself and start anew.

That day wouldn't be today, though. Rob turned the page without so much as a sigh, refusing to give the men in the truck anything to be suspicious about. For now, they still followed him, even when he couldn't explain why. He was confident that the next entry in the journal would give him just the reason to trust in what he was about to try and pull off. With the air conditioning blowing on his face and the sun's warmth filling his cheeks, he turned the page and allowed himself to sink into yet another tale.

August 10, 1881

169

This is what legends are made of. The boss proved to the nation itself why his name is printed on wanted posters and in the pages of dime novels. At long last, I finally understood why I'd signed my own life away to run from the law with the handful of men who followed that man. We all thought a bank robbery was without a doubt the worst idea possible at a time when we were being hunted down like dogs in the street. As fortune would have it, such a brazen act of stupidity and courage proved to be the one thing no one expected. We walked into a bank just off the banks of the Big Muddy. We didn't need to say who we were or what we wanted. We handed over a couple of sacks, and the tellers went to work giving away everything of value stored inside those four walls. Behind the rags covering our faces, there were big smiles on the lot of us. The boss didn't do any dirty work for this one, but he showed why his was the name everyone knew far and wide. I hope one day to fill those shoes, to have my name printed on anything that will take the ink. We made enough to cover our troubles for the rest of the year, but we are only taking a few months to go our separate ways. Well, at least everyone but Charlie. The poor idiot. They say the chances of being struck down by your own bullet are next to nothing. Charlie must've been standing right next to the Grim Reaper himself, then. The warning shot he fired into the air ricocheted off the wall and came right back to him before he knew what happened. I still remember the look on his face when he hit the ground. He was dead, but he was shocked, too. I'll all drink to his name tonight, likely as I parse through the latest correspondence from the Governor...

Bob.

When Rob lifted his eyes from the cracked and

creased page of the journal, he saw the same highway they'd been driving for the last hour. It was monotonous. O'Kelley only let out an occasional sniffle of blood still trying to run from his nose, and the new guy hadn't done so much as cough since they left. This was usually the time when he'd pick Sam's brain about their circumstance, ask questions about what they should do next, or even what they planned to do after they were free from the grasp of the Bossman.

This time, Sam and Rob shared only a passing, worrying glance. Each had their own reason. Rob, because he wasn't quite sure if the plan rolling around in his head would work, and if it did, who might wind up dead because of it. Sam, because he knew the man sitting directly behind Rob in the backseat was a lying, traitorous man who didn't deserve the oxygen in his lungs. The awkwardness hit Rob like a ton of bricks, so he did the only thing he could to put a stop to it.

"A thousand head would pay off our debts," he said. "Well, everyone except you, Bill."

The new guy had nothing to say, for reasons that were most likely to remain his own.

"The way I see it, no one said anything about where they had to be from. I know we thought the Coleman Ranch was gonna be our ticket to freedom, but I'm starting to think we weren't all that wrong."

Sam didn't take his eyes off the road when he spoke. "What does that mean?"

"It means we gotta find a thousand head if we want to have a leg to stand on when we tell Bossman we want out from under his boot."

"You just said it, though, we blew our shot at it. Didn't even get started before we were droppin' like flies," said Sam.

"Tell us what to do," O'Kelley grunted, in opposition of the man who'd beaten him half to death.

"The Coleman Ranch has used the same sale barn for about twenty years now. Most places follow the money, haul their cattle wherever they need to go just to make a few more cents on the pound. Not the Colemans."

"How do you know where they go?"

"Everyone knows where they go, but what they don't know is that the Colemans own that whole damn place," said Rob. "Panola Auction got sold a couple years back, and when it looked like some rich family coming out of New York City was going to scoop it up, the Colemans bought it themselves through a proxy. The owner is an employee of the head honcho down at the Coleman Ranch."

"No shit?" O'Kelley couldn't stop the comment before it left his mouth.

"No shit," Rob confirmed.

"Are you saying we're going to hit a sale barn?" Sam asked in between changing lanes on the highway.

Rob finally turned to look at him before he spoke, and then said, "Yes, sir, that's exactly what we're gonna do."

The next few minutes saw Rob making a phone call to the anonymous number given to him when he first started running the outfit. It was the only way to set up a drop-off for Bossman's crew to swap the EID tags and change the tattoos before re-registering the cattle to whatever shell ranch was being used at the time. Without this step, there was nothing that could be done. The only problem was that it was usually initiated by Bossman himself. When word came down through the grapevine about who they were supposed to be hitting next, the phone call would be a simple confirmation of what had already been scheduled. This time, Rob caught them off guard, and for a few minutes, he thought it might not be possible.

By the time the phone call came to an end, Rob had set up the first job that was conceived and planned by him alone. The Panola sale barn might have once been a hole in the wall that ran maybe a hundred head a week in front of half a dozen buyers, but since the Colemans took over, it was an undeniable powerhouse that ran more than sixty thousand head through the sale last year alone. That meant more than a thousand head per week, exactly what Rob and the outfit needed to make up for what had happened just a few nights before, when Hicks and Cliff were gunned down in their failure.

"Take this exit," Rob finally said.

The truck veered off to the right and they sped down the farm road in hurry, bypassing a couple of stop signs that only about half of drivers ever came to a stop at. They were no more than ten minutes away from the Panola sale barn.

"They have a sale every Thursday," Rob explained. "There'll be a line damn near fifteen miles down Highway 79 in the morning. We won't get those, but there should be plenty already waiting in the barn for us."

"Ain't there someone who watches over all them? Hard to imagine everyone just goes home with all that money standin' around," said Sam.

"There's one guy who stays in the shack around back where they unload trailers. We deal with him and we're all set."

"You make it sound so easy."

"I don't see why it can't be."

"What's the catch?"

At this point, Sam and Rob had left out both of the men sitting in the backseat. It had gone back to the old ways in just a matter of minutes, and it was something Rob took inexplicable comfort in. They had found success in these small talks in the truck. It felt like the calm before the storm.

"Bossman doesn't know it's happening," Rob admitted. "If we pull it off, there's nothing he can say."

"And if we don't?"

"We're every bit as screwed as we are now."

"Well, in that case..." Sam allowed his voice to trail off as he became lost in his thoughts.

"I ain't dying over this," the new guy chimed in. "Just so you know."

"You're welcome to sit it out," Rob said without looking back at him. "But don't expect any cut of the cash to go toward your debt. I'll be sure you get exactly what you give—nothing. Just so *you know*."

Silence fell over the cabin after Rob's warning. They rode along without saying a word until the Panola sale barn appeared as a looming shadow in the distance, a promised solution to all of their problems hidden in the night, waiting for them to only show up and take what was waiting for them.

The building had become a far cry from its heyday, despite selling more cattle every week than it ever had. It wasn't run-down, yet, but it was sure on its way. The office out front had been remodeled a couple years back, but the pens and the walkway overhead had certainly seen better days. In the darkness, it looked like a twisted mess of steel and wire and dirt, but Rob knew it was a gold mine waiting to be tapped.

"Pull around back," he said with a wag of his finger, leaning up in his seat to get a better look into the black wall in the night surrounding the sale barn.

When the truck eased into the lane used for unloading trailers at the back of the barn, it didn't take long for things to turn serious. There was a line of eighteen-wheelers parked diligently alongside the border of the property. The diesel engines hummed steadily like a rose bush in spring coated in bees, but there were no lights on or drivers to be seen. Rob stared them down as he walked into the single lane in the separating rows of pens crammed full of bellering cattle donning yellow, numbered stickers tossed haphazardly onto their hips.

Sam, O'Kelly, and Bill all followed closely behind him, waiting patiently on the word to begin their work. It was dusty inside the old barn, and it smelled of cow shit and piss building up over years of grime, but to Rob, it smelled like a million bucks.

"Easy cowboyin' tonight y'all," he said, with a wink before lifting his hands. "Let's load 'em up!" Rob screamed to the eighteen-wheelers, motioning for them to start pulling into the loading bay.

"We just supposed to run all these head into the trailers?" Bill asked with a dumbfounded look on his face.

"You got any better ideas?"

As the steel gates started to creak and swing open, Sam and O'Kelley quietly went to work. It was a sight to see from Rob's perspective. Hooves sending dirt into a swirling cloud only to be lost in the night air, a sea of horns and tails swaying in unison, bright yellow stickers as far as the eye could see totaling thousands of dollars a piece, and eighteen-wheelers with trailers ready to haul every head away. There must have been thirty semi-trucks moving through the back of the sale barn, lined up with pens on either side as far as the eye could see at such a time of night. It was magnificent, and it made Rob swell with pride for one of the only times in his life he'd known such a feeling.

For the man the locals knew only as *Buck*, it was a horrific, unbelievable sight that made his heart fall into the bottom of his gut.

Rob knew there was always someone who stayed around to help unload in a hurry, but he never would have guessed that man would have the kind of blind confidence that would send him sprinting into their outfit without so much as a closed fist to defend himself. Rob watched as the man—dressed in an unbuttoned flannel, jeans that hadn't been washed in days, and a stained cap barely resting on his head—came running through a partially opened steel gate, hollering something about how no one was allowed in the sale barn right now.

No one stopped what they were doing. Cattle poured into the back of trailers like water flowing from a well. What had started couldn't be stopped, especially not by the likes of men like Buck who'd spent their honest lives just trying to get by. He was doing the right thing, but he had finally found the wrong people.

It was the new guy, Bill, who raised his gun first. Rob didn't know where he got it, but it was painfully obvious he'd never shot it before. Bill's intention was to fire a warning shot into the air, that much was plain as the day sure to come—but it wasn't what happened. The new guy fumbled his draw, panicked to hold the snub-nose revolver with any control, and jerked the trigger back before it was even pointed up at the sky. A bullet ripped through Bill's neck, tore out his trachea with a splatter of blood, and sent the man gurgling on his own insides in the dirt.

"What the fu—"

"Get the hell out of here!"

Bam. Bam. Bam.

The sale barn hand tried his best to get away, but a bullet fired by O'Kelley pierced his back and exited through his stomach, sending him collapsing to the ground, screaming for help and clawing to get away by any means necessary.

"Nobody else fire a damn gun! You're gonna get the cops called out here if you haven't already," Rob hollered over everything going on.

Poor Buck didn't stand a chance. His meager, yet meaningful life, had been cut short unnecessarily, and there wasn't anything Rob could do about that. He had a feeling that man's death would be coming back to haunt him one way or another. As cattle darted all around him, he watched the man crawl no more than ten yards in the dirt and manure before going still and finally letting his head sink to the ground.

Two people were dead in a matter of minutes. Two more were lost from the outfit. Two more men's blood was on Rob's hands. His palms were stained red at this point, and it was starting to take its toll. Death weighed heavier to those standing beneath the rotting walkway, surrounded by rusted steel pipe and sucker rod fencing that made up the livestock auction. Whether it was bovine or human, the place welcomed the Grim Reaper with open arms and open wallets.

A chill worked its way from the top of Rob's spine and all the way down. Sam and O'Kelley were the only professionals in the group, and they did what they did best—finished the job. While big rigs cycled in and out of the back of the sale barn to the tune of Sam and O'Kelley yipping and hollering to push the cattle forward into every single one of the never-ending line of trailers. Rob thought only of the man in the journal who was killed by his own bullet, and he wondered if he had single-handedly gotten Bill killed. To what end would he chase the words in the journal in his own life?

A wannabe cowboy, a real-life outlaw, a man with a penchant for cowboys and singing, even a dreamer of a better life, but the government would call him only one thing if he was to ever fail—a murderer.

There was no going back. Even if one sale barn cleaned out wasn't enough to wipe their debt from existence, the next one would. The sinking pain in the bottom of his belly wasn't enough to turn him away from what had to be done. Whether the cost of his freedom was four men, or forty men, it was a cost Rob would pay to finally run away from his own life.

It was the final trailer door slamming shut which snapped Rob from the void and back into a reality where what he wanted most was within his grasp at last.

"We got ourselves an old-fashioned cattle haul," Rob said with a smirk. He walked by the body of Bill first, without so much as a passing glance, then the body of Buck next, affording him a slight nod of his head for his unwilling sacrifice.

"Think it's enough?" Sam asked.

"Ain't no way," O'Kelley smarted off through swollen lips and a black eye.

"Only one way to find out." Rob pulled out his cell phone and pushed it to the side of his face. After a few empty seconds waiting on someone to pick up the phone from the latest anonymous number he'd been given, Rob finally spoke to whoever was on the other end of the line.

"Tell Bossman it's time to meet."

Chapter 17

There are some lines people don't cross.

Belief in a God that is not their own or refusing a drink of cool water when on the brink of dehydration are among them, but an employee meeting his employer should never be. It is a line that exists metaphorically, and anything less is simply a disservice to the mission at hand. Even so, there isn't a cure in the world for the feeling that overcomes the human mind when sitting across from a boss you so desperately hope to receive something from. Whether it's a few more dollars for an hour of your life or your very freedom, the same feeling is there.

Going to meet the Bossman for the first time face-to-face, dragged on longer than crossing Texas itself, a state that is seven hundred and seventy-three miles wide and takes two days to drive across. It was this long of a trip that Rob had to sit with the feeling of what the man who owned his debt would say to him when they finally looked one another dead in the eye. He thought about what he would say as well, but even he knew better than to speak out of turn when everything he could ever want rested in a single man's greedy, vengeful hands.

He had found himself back in the same truck he'd always found himself in, sitting next to Sam, who was driving them down the highway, doing eighty-five in a seventy-mile-an-hour speed limit area. O'Kelley had chosen to ride with the trailers to ensure nothing else happened to them in the haul to the drop-off. He said he'd catch up to them for their meeting, and Rob didn't argue. There was only a few minutes of silence between the two. Rob wasn't in the mood to listen to the diesel engine haul ass down the highway. He didn't want to hear music through the speakers or even the words of the journal whisper into his mind.

Rob had a question for Sam that he just couldn't wait to ask, "Should we have killed O'Kelley when we had the chance?"

"Of course we should have."

"What if you're wrong? Hogtie, Hicks, Cliff, and now Bill. We're dyin' quicker than we can be replaced. If the Bossman can't find enough bodies to hurl down the grinder, maybe it's us."

"There's a reason they're dead and we ain't, Robbie."

"I'm saying, what if that reason is us?"

"Don't really matter," said Sam, refusing to take his eyes off the road like he so often did when speaking. "Only thing that matters is we're still suckin' air."

"That's what I thought when I started all this," Rob admitted. "I'm not so sure anymore."

"We all signed the same contract. We all know what it is. It's a *get out of a jail free* card, except it ain't free. We're in debt with the Bossman for what he did for us. Once we pay him back, he gives us our freedom back. Anything that ain't about us repaying our debt and taking back our freedom is a waste of time."

"Who do you want to be when you don't have to work for that man?"

"What does that mean?" Sam asked, glancing to the side for a split second, hoping Rob wouldn't notice.

"You know what it means," said Rob. "The way I'm feeling, I am thinking about gunning them all down and making a run for it."

"Why haven't you?"

"Remember those kids back before we went into the Coleman Ranch?"

Sam nodded, but it wasn't enough to convince Rob he understood what was going on.

"If he's tracking children, we're all screwed no matter what happens. I've been thinking a lot about the kind of man we work for, and maybe he does deserve to die."

"Not to get all philosophical or nothing, but don't we all?"

"Not like him."

The truck fell into silence. They both knew that O'Kelley wasn't worth keeping alive, and they both were trying their damndest to hold onto some semblance of morality despite not wanting to talk about it. Deep down, they feared the simple fact that if everyone had to die, that meant they'd be staring down the barrel of each other's guns one way or another.

It should have stayed silent. They should have remained in their thoughts and maintained an understanding that sharing too much would be too dangerous. Their situation was too unpredictable, and the man they called boss was almost certainly in bed with the worst kind of people the world had to offer. Everything they did had to be strategic, even when it was with someone they thought they trusted.

"So, what did your dad do to get you in all this mess?"

"He did enough to earn that bullet, I can guarantee that."

"I don't doubt it," said Sam. "You never said why you killed him, though."

"And you never said anything about why you were stuck next to me stealing cattle. How long's it been? Hell, I've been a wide open book compared to you."

Sam let out one of the only smiles Rob had ever seen from the man. "Well, to be fair, you never asked."

"I'm askin' now."

It was a gentleman's barter, one with an underlying belief that they would be exchanging more than information. It was about anything that would make pulling that trigger just a little bit more difficult when the time came. It was about making a choice when there were so few to be made.

"Not much to it, bein' completely honest," Sam started. "My momma had been dealing with this guy on and off again for a couple of years. It never went nowhere. He didn't agree with it. One day, they were fighting over money or some shit, things went south, and one cuss word turned into another. Before anyone knew what was happening, he was standin' over her like the trash he was."

"So you killed a guy, too, huh?"

"Sure did," Sam said with a newfound sense of confidence in his words. "The only problem was, I showed up too late."

"What does that mean?"

"It means none of the courts could call it self-defense. They told me to my face I gunned that man down in cold blood. It took one lawyer with one cryin' supposed relative to make me out to be the monster in the whole situation. Didn't matter how many black eyes my momma got, didn't matter how many times she got put in the hospital and the cops got called out for domestic violence, the only thing that mattered were those ninety seconds it took me to kick the door down and rack the slide of that damn pistol."

"How did you get out of all that if you were already arrested?"

"I was about ten days into my fifteen-year sentence—about to be transferred out of the county jail and into a federal prison—when a jailer walked up to his confinement cell and pulled out a key. Next thing I know, I'm walkin' free out the front doors wonderin' what in the hell I did to deserve such a fate."

"No shit?"

"That's right," Sam said with a smile that faded into hateful, bitter resentment. "That's when I saw him, standin' across the street with his hands in his pockets. It was like he was mocking me, like his pockets were empty because of me, and it was my job to fix it."

Sam gripped the steering wheel a little tighter. The worn leather creaked against his tightening grasp just as his jaw clenched and his teeth grinded together in frustration.

"I signed that contract so I didn't have to spend my best years locked away. I know everyone says it, but I was innocent when it came to self-defense. That man would've never stopped until my momma then me was dead. Simple as that."

"I don't doubt it for one second."

"This place likes to lock up men who look like me, though. So, I didn't have much of a choice either way. I figured I'd rather work my way to freedom than sit on my ass."

Rob finally let out a chuckle. He wasn't laughing at Sam's situation, only the fact that it took a certain kind of man to pull off what they were doing—and he fit the mold damn near perfectly.

"You gave it more thought than I ever did," Rob said.

"You gonna tell me what it was all about, now?"

"Not much to tell, bein' completely honest."

"Don't you give me that shit now, not after I just got done telling you my whole damn life story."

"That's the whole thing, I'd have to tell you my whole life story for you to understand why I pulled the trigger when I did. It wasn't just one thing."

"You killed your dad over a bunch of little things? You just explode one day and gun him down for calling you a jackoff or something?"

"Screw you," Rob shot back with a smirk.

"He ever hit you?"

"Hell, I struggle to remember the days he didn't."

"He ever steal from you?"

"How do you think I learned how to do it?"

"Drink?"

"Smoked," said Rob. "Anything and everything he could get his hands on."

"Yeah," Sam agreed with where Rob was going with his story already. "I know the types."

"He always told me he gave me the name of a coward because he knew deep down who I was right when I was born. Always told me just get used to runnin' because that's all I'd ever do. It's like putting me down was his whole reason for being. Cussin' and spittin' at me eventually turned to beatin' and stealin' from me, but it didn't stop there."

"So, you're one of those guys, huh?"

"What's that supposed to mean?"

"You're innocent. It wasn't your fault. You're just a misunderstood victim in all this. Makes you the hero in your own story, or at the very least, not the bad guy."

"I never said any of that." Rob let his eyes fall to the floorboard of the pickup as he contemplated how to find the words for someone else's ears. Sometimes it still sounded foreign to himself, and it wasn't really something he spoke about often—or at all. "When I found out I wasn't the only kid he was doing that to, that those hands of his had a reputation only the worst scum of the world could hope to match, it made what I did pretty easy. Even so, that don't mean I didn't deserve everything that happened to me. He may have earned that bullet, but I earned my own consequences. That's why I turned myself in right after everything happened."

"That's where the Bossman scooped you up?"

"Pretty much," said Rob, finally letting his eyes look up from his muddy boots. "He was my way out of the only life I'd ever known. His only promise was that I'd have to live it for just a few more years, so he could get ahead. Whatever that means."

"It means you won't ever get away," said Sam. "Same as it means for me."

"Did you get the numbers speech?"

"About a thousand head?"

"That's the one," Rob chuckled as he spoke. "One thousand head at a dollar eighty-five a pound—"

"Is just enough to buy your freedom back from

those who stole it from you," Sam completed his sentence while shaking his head in disbelief.

"And that's low!" Rob mimicked the Bossman's speech.

"Market is just gonna keep climbing!" Sam did the same.

"Hard to believe we signed our lives away to make this guy millions while we barely avoid getting killed in the process. Whole damn thing makes me want to run away from it all and never look back."

"Even harder to believe he'll ever let his main source of income just walk free."

"One way or another, we're about to find out."

Their drive ended in yet another secluded area somewhere out in the woods. It was pines and oaks and brush so thick you couldn't see more than ten feet away, just like it was everywhere else, but there was something else in the clearing they had rolled into. It was heavy. The air had a chill that went down Rob's spine, and his breath shuddered before he could even climb out of the pickup. Scraggly limbs reached out overhead, tangling with one another in an impossible struggle for life, illuminated only by the moonlight creeping through cracks and crevices.

It was this very moonlight that Rob found himself basking in as he waited for an inevitable man he'd come to know simply as the *Bossman*. He told Sam about his contract, about how he'd gotten himself in yet another situation he couldn't run from, but he never said anything about the fact that he'd never actually met the man who held their reins. His entire future rested in the hands of a faceless businessman who couldn't even be bothered to shake his hand like a real man.

All of that was about to change. He'd done what he needed to do. He'd turned in more than a thousand head to Bossman, and he never asked a single time about where all that money went. He didn't care. All he wanted was to get away, to run as fast as he could, but he refused to do it before knowing he wouldn't get shot in the back the second he turned around. Now that he had paid his dues, the only question that remained was where the keys to his shackles truly lied? Anything less than that would be a validation of his, and Sam's, worst nightmare. Neither wanted to believe they'd never be released of their servitude, but until they were walking free, it would always be a possibility they'd have to prepare for.

There wasn't a particular vision Rob had in mind for what Bossman could look like. When it came down to it, he only ever imagined a man who'd collected all of his money. He was a man who paid no attention to the needs of others, cared only about his own whims, and thought nothing of what others may be going through. From what Rob knew of him, that could be anyone. He expected a menace, someone with eyes that could hide the depravity of the soul. He expected a man forsaken by even himself, embraced only by the things most sane people would never even come to know. That is not what he found waiting on him in the woods.

The diesel engine roared a final time before it was killed, leaving behind the chaos known only to the grasshoppers, cicadas, limpkins, toads, owls, foxes, coyotes, raccoons, and whip-poor-wills. Their combined screeches rose and fell like the swell of a tide guided by the same moonlight Rob used tonight to find his way face-to-face with the one thing he wanted most —freedom.

He'd welcomed the recent distraction from the feelings of terror and anxiety that danced together in his chest. As he laid his eyes on the hulking silhouette of a man with broad shoulders, oversized gut, and a cowboy hat Hopalong Cassidy himself would be proud of, he felt the all too familiar feeling once again rise into his throat. It was suffocating. It demanded everything he had. Cowardice consumed him. If he didn't know any better, he would've guaranteed his knees were knocking with every step he took closer to the only one who could let him do what he wanted most.

"Where's O'Kelley?"

Before Rob could even lay his eyes on the man hidden by the shadows of night, he'd been dumbfounded by the first words out of his mouth. They were impossible to register. After all that, those were the words he'd first hear out of Bossman's mouth?

"Where the hell is he?"

"He ain't here?" Sam said, buying Rob a few more seconds to get his bearings.

"You think I'm stupid, boy?"

"Well, he was in front of us. I don't know why he ain't here yet."

Rob finally shook himself back to his senses and spoke up. "You know why we're here, Bossman?"

"I'll talk to you when I'm good and ready."

Rob took one more step and watched as the man who towered above him like the pines that surrounded them came into view beneath faint traces of moonlight. His bushy beard and black eyes were shadows in the night, but his stature said everything. It was a man who knew what power felt like and wasn't afraid to wield it aimlessly. Anyone who got in the line of fire would be of no consequence to him. Instead of feeling like an equal, or at the very least an employee, Rob felt only like an acceptable casualty.

"And the name is Woodson," the man across from Rob said. "Mr. Woodson to you."

"Yes, sir," Rob said without thinking.

Just as Rob and Sam lined up side by side in front of Mr. Woodson, another vehicle came rolling into the clearing in the trees. The door flew open, and a beaming O'Kelley hopped out with a unique pep in his step. His pearly whites glinted in the moon as he raised his hand in the air above his head and started shouting.

"Mr. Woodson! I'm not late, I promise!" O'Kelley said. "You're just early!"

Rob watched in silent shock as Mr. Woodson let out a chuckle and motioned him over to where Rob and Sam were standing. It was an awkward few seconds waiting on him, but nothing compared to the dread Rob was feeling as he waited on his boss to acknowledge their recent attempts to buy their freedom.

O'Kelley lined up without saying another word, yet still refusing to wipe that shit-eating grin off of his face. Mr. Woodson gave the man Sam and Rob suspected of being the rat a pat on the shoulder before turning his attention to Rob.

"Whose bright idea was it?"

Rob hesitated to take the credit, glancing at Sam to find that he was doing the same thing.

"Cut that shit out and tell me," said Mr. Woodson.

"It was me," said Rob.

"The head honcho himself, huh?" Mr. Woodson

took a step closer. "So, let me guess. You think you just turned in your get out of jail free card with that thousand head you ransacked and dumped off to my guys."

"I failed back at the Colemans' place," Rob started to explain. "This was me making up for that, plus interest."

"Is that right?"

"Yes, sir. It just so happened to be all that was left on mine and Sam's contract with you. So, we were thinking—"

"Oh!" Mr. Woodson exclaimed. "You two were thinking? Well, I don't know about you two, but that sure as *shit* surprises me." The boss took another step closer, coming to within inches of Rob's face. "Just a few days away from the auction that will change all of our lives, the one I have every goddam thing riding on, and you two decide to chase some bright idea to risk it all. I was gonna hold that auction right where you're standing, but now I'm starting to think I'm gonna hold it on top of your dead bodies buried in the mud."

Rob could smell the cigar smoke still lingering in his lungs, the tobacco traces escaping from his gums, and the sweaty musk pouring from his skin as he leaned in close. For a brief moment, Rob wondered if he was about to take a strike to the jaw, the likes of which he wanted to give O'Kelley right about now. Instead of a closed fist, Rob was met with an open hand that smacked him so hard, he was down on his knees before he knew what hit him.

"You think you run this, you piece of shit? You think you can do whatever you want? You think you can tell me what to do? You think you can *walk away* whenever you want?" Mr. Woodson was screaming so loud his voice echoed off the trees for what seemed like miles in every direction. "Look at me, you son of a bitch. I'm gonna let you in on something you ain't quite figured out, yet."

Rob finally got the stomach to look up at his boss looming over him, still shouting so hard his face had turned beet-red and his veins were bulging from his neck. He winced at the pain in his jaw before Mr. Woodson leaned in a little closer and spoke through his teeth.

"I fuckin' *own* you!"

Chapter 18

"If we don't get out of this, we're gonna die."

Rob was as serious as a heart attack. His eyes were misty and his cheeks were flushed. He'd dwelled on the words of the man he now knew as Mr. Woodson all night long, unable to think about anything other than those four words spoken through snuff-filled teeth and filled with deadly animosity matched only by the venom of a pissed off cottonmouth. Those words rattled around in his head until they had almost lost all meaning. Almost. By the time the sun started to rise, he was ready to do whatever it took to get out from beneath that man's boot.

They had left O'Kelley behind, not by their own will, but because they were told to leave after Mr. Woodson had raged at both Sam and Rob for no less than half an hour. Rob's jaw may have been bruised, but his ego was far from it. If he ever hoped to run from this life, he would have to do it the hard way—through threats and blood and gunpowder. If he could get Sam on board without giving away his intentions to O'Kelley, he might have a chance of pulling it off.

He would never confide in Sam about what he'd discovered in the pages of the journal he still carried around, but he knew beyond a shadow of a doubt that it would give him just the edge he needed.

Judging by the look on Sam's face, it would take a lot more than just some far-fetched theory that would require any sort of leap of faith. Rob knew it didn't matter what the journal would say, but he knew there was something else that would give them leverage against Mr. Woodson.

"We can't buy our way out, and we can't steal our way out," Rob continued. "The only thing chasing any of that is gonna do is get us killed."

"Might as well face the reality," Sam finally answered. "You can't run away from things like justice. They have a way of creeping back up on you."

"We aren't the ones who need to face reality."

"You said it yourself, you deserve every single thing that has come your way because of your own actions. No one else's."

"We all have to face the music one way or another," said Rob. "I don't disagree with anything you're saying. I'm trying to tell you it's the Bossman's turn."

"You really want to take him on? Think about the people he hangs around with and what they get up to with all that money."

"I'm thinking about all those poor kids we ran into back at the Colemans. I'm thinking about what else was back where they escaped—or who else was back there."

Sam stopped arguing for just a few seconds to think about what Rob was telling him. He remembered the look in their eyes and wondered what exactly they were being put through. He tried to consider any possibility other than the obvious, and tried even harder to ignore the role he played in enabling it.

"Shit," was all he could let out.

Rob knew it wasn't something anyone wanted to consider. After one failure turned into another, it was impossible not to reflect on them. That was where both of the rustling hands found themselves inside yet another safe house they'd never seen before. This time, it was a metal building with no insulation and only enough plumbing tucked away in one corner for a kitchen sink and a bathroom toilet. It was almost entirely open inside. It was cold and illuminated by overhead fluorescent lighting. The concrete slab floor was stained with oil and remnants of paint, and the only insulation to be found inside the building had been sprayed on along the ceiling rafters and decking years ago.

"We all tried to ignore it, and we'll pay the price for that one day," Rob continued. "But if we had any sense of decency, we'd have turned around and gone back for whoever didn't make it out with the rest. That's still true right now, too."

"You ain't wrong," Sam admitted.

"Who we tell about it is still up to us, though."

"What are you trying to say?"

"I'm saying we go take anything we can get our hands on and use it as our ticket out of this life."

"Why in the hell would he let us live after that?"

"You know how blackmail works, right? He won't be able to harm a single hair on our heads. We're gonna have his nuts in a pair of vice grips. He'll have no choice but to do whatever we want or we'll burn everything to the ground on our way out."

"I know it's the right thing to do," said Sam. "But there is pretty much zero percent chance we walk away from that."

"I don't plan on walking away. I'm planning on running away."

"We need a plan, we can't just barge in. And we need to figure out what is going to happen with O'Kelley."

"That fuckin' guy," Rob tried to mutter under his breath.

"He's gunnin' for your job," said Sam. "You could see it in his eyes when that Woodson asshole was there."

"Yeah, I'm aware."

"And from how Bossman was treating you, O'Kelley might be on to something."

"I'm aware of that, too. All any of that means to me is that we're running out of time in a hurry."

"Well, you got a plan?"

Rob knew this was where he'd lose Sam. He couldn't afford to tell him about Robert Ford's journal, how it was predicting the future, and by proxy, keeping him alive. It sounded crazy in his head, and he shuddered to think about how those words would sound coming from his own mouth. He needed to read the next entry to find any semblance of an idea about how to take the fight to Mr. Woodson.

If he was a smart man, he would've had a well-prepared explanation for exactly what they were about to try and pull off. He could have presented its complexity and likened it to a heist for a train full of gold. He could have blown Sam away with contingencies and variables that would just about guarantee their success. Ultimately, though, Rob was a simple man and he lived his life on simple, honest terms.

"Give me a second," was the best he could come up with before scurrying away behind a closed door, trying not to be conspicuous.

The door slamming shut was all he needed to know it was safe to whip out the journal and pour everything he had into it in the hopes of finding answers to questions he didn't even know to ask. Its musty pages and scribbled handwriting were no different than the warmth of sunlight washing over him after a cold morning doing chores. His eyes danced across the swoops and curves of stories that had already come to pass, careful not to get too far ahead and risk everything he'd come to know of its potential.

His fingers trembled as his thoughts raced. The look on the children's faces and the feeling of Mr. Woodson's calloused hand striking him played over and over again in his mind. If he couldn't work his way out just like he agreed, and he couldn't run away from a life that would only follow him wherever he went, then he'd have to run toward something else.

He only needed to know where.

November 28, 1881

    I've been alone for more weeks than I could keep count of. My time with the gang seems like it had come and gone a lifetime ago, leaving me hopelessly in despair. I've found day work here and there, enough to get by. I'm tired of getting by. I joined up with my brother and that man to do more than all that. I was supposed to be someone, supposed to learn from the legend and forge my own. He hasn't spoken to me since that Big Muddy bank robbery, neither has my brother. No one has so much as written from that life I can barely come to terms with now. If I try real hard, I can almost pretend it didn't happen, or that I was one of the few who got away in time to grow old. Most times I don't try too hard, though. Didn't have much of a reason to pick up a pen and paper all this time, not until I finally did get a letter. The Governor always has a way of finding me, no matter where I go. He says some things have changed, and that I could find it more than lucrative to sit down with him. Says my boss's days are numbered and mine are too. This time, I wrote him back. That's how I found out my boss had someone watching me. They surrounded me on the way to drop off the letter, but they didn't get it from me. There might have been three of them, but I already knew how firepower can even the odds. I learned it from the same man who set them all upon me. I may have six less bullets than I had this morning, but I will be going to bed tonight to dream of a life of riches and renown purchased by that same gunpowder and lead, written into a pact with the Governor himself. All I have to do is squeeze that trigger one more time and gun down the man who taught me everything I know. I'd rather be known as the man who killed a myth than not be known at all.

Bob.

"What the—"

Rob's heart was sinking deep into his stomach as he whispered a string of expletives. He had no chance of gunning down Mr. Woodson if he wanted to get out alive. It was senseless to think he could get close enough to his boss to do anything after what he'd just gone through. And there certainly was no plea bargain from law enforcement he could turn to. The upper edge he needed now more than ever before was to turn himself in—to become a rat?

He shook his head to clear the thoughts rattling around, and began to consider the reckless abandon it would take to do what the journal was suggesting. He was an idiot for even giving it the time of day, but it was all he had. For a moment, he even thought about ignoring its words, pretending it was just the ramblings of a long-dead outlaw-turned-traitor. He couldn't lie to himself, though. He knew in his bones there was some-thing more to the legacy of the man who killed Jesse James, there was something that miraculously connected them through time, against all odds, and in defiance of natural law. It wasn't something he could ignore at this point, and his only option was to chase it and discover its meaning.

There are essentially no circumstances where contacting the authorities would be an advisable thing to do for a man in Rob's position. It just didn't make sense. Without any redeeming qualities or leverage, without any chips to bargain with, there would be no resolution to be found with the cops that wouldn't lead to Rob's own downfall. He didn't know a single soul with a halfway-functioning brain would ever tell him to dial the sheriff's number on the smudged and cracked screen of his smartphone. Every time his thumb smashed a number on the screen, he conjured up another question of his own sanity, and by the time he heard the ringing on the other line in its speaker pressed against his face, he concluded he'd lost it entirely sometime long ago.

"Hello?" A grizzled voice came through the other end.

"Sheriff," said Rob. "You may not know who I am, but you've been chasin' me long enough to know just about everything about me."

"I know who you are."

"Do you know what that man is up to?"

"I do."

"Then you must not have what you need to stop him. If you did, it would have already been done by now, and I wouldn't be in this mess."

"No, you wouldn't," said the sheriff. "You'd be sitting behind bars staring at me right now."

"I can tell you where the children are," Rob said in a heavy voice. "That should be all you need."

"You'd think it would be, but it ain't. You're gonna have to do better than that."

"Shit."

There was an awkward silence that worked its way into the phone call, filled only by the white noise of the connection and an occasional breath picked up by the microphone. Rob wasn't sure if he should say what he was thinking, but he didn't have much else to give. If he wanted to turn the tide against his boss, he'd have to hit him where it hurts. And if he wanted to follow the words he'd just read in the journal, if there was any truth to them at all, it would take him speaking to this man.

"There's an auction coming up," Rob started to explain, going against every bone in his body, screaming to shut the hell up. "He's all kinds of stressed about it. Told me himself everything was on the line."

"When is it?"

"Coming up quick."

"Where is it?"

"Not too far from you."

"You're gonna have to give me a heck of a lot more than that, buddy. I know things you don't even know. If you're gonna rat him out, just go on and get it over with so we can get to work. If you don't give me anything, I promise when I catch you—not *if*—I will bury your ass under the jail without a second thought. If you give me something, though, I might think otherwise."

"What do you mean you know things?"

"That's what you took away from all that? Maybe you're just slow. That'd sure explain a lot."

Rob hesitated for a second before a swear escaped beneath his breath.

"Go on," said the sheriff. "Give it up."

"You remember where they found that guy in the trunk of a sedan out in the woods off the highway a couple years back? What was his name…" Rob trailed off.

"Jack?" The sheriff knew exactly what he was talking about. "Jack Richards, the insurance agent, homicide."

"That's the one. Go about a mile and a half down the road, and it's on your right."

"That's just a patch of woods. You think I don't know my own county?"

"So, you don't need me to tell you about the oil company that just bought the mineral rights a couple years ago, and how that same family is one of that man's biggest clients. And you probably already know what they're getting in exchange for allowing that auction to take place on their location? Hell, you're probably getting a cut too. Y'all are enabling one of the largest narco ranching operations in the world. Letting them do whatever they want, whenever they want, whether it's trafficking kids or running drugs. It's all right in your backyard, sheriff. Did you know that about *your* county?"

"That's enough, smartass," said the sheriff.

"You need to stop him. That's all there is to it. And when you do, don't plan on seein' my face anywhere nearby."

"I better not."

"I ain't a bad person," Rob tried to explain himself for reasons he didn't understand, to a man he didn't even respect. The words came out of him nonetheless, as foreign and sour-tasting as anything he's ever uttered. "I just got roped into the wrong shit at the wrong time."

"That's what they all say," said the sheriff.

An empty dial tone took over the call, becoming a flatline that would be the end of a life Rob never wanted for himself.

Chapter 19

"*That* was your big plan?"

There wasn't much of a discussion between Sam and Rob to be had after that call with the sheriff. Sam had taken it about as well as anyone would in his position, which was to say he was about as pissed off as a wet hen. As Rob was explaining the conversation to him, he could see the poor man's face turn from disbelief to justified fury with every passing word. It had to be done, but Rob couldn't tell him why. All he could do was ask for a trust that he hadn't earned.

They were back in the truck, ready to tear each other's throats out, but unable to do anything except what was necessary. They may have agreed on where they were going, but when Sam found out what Rob had done, they were about as far apart as possible on how exactly they'd get there. It'd taken some time to game-plan their next steps. It wasn't going to be easy to disrupt Mr. Woodson's upcoming auction with the slightest inconvenience, much less send the whole thing down in a ball of fire just before the authorities could find them. It could be done, though, and it was all thanks to the gumption of those children on the run, escaping a life they would not accept.

"I ain't the sharpest tool in the shed, Rob, you know that," said Sam, as Rob nodded silently in agreement. "But I know a dumbass idea when I see it, and that right there was a dumbass idea."

"You might be right."

"I know I'm right. Telling the cops is the opposite of what we wanna ever do. That means our days are numbered. Is that what you want?"

"No, it sure ain't. What I want is for Bossman's days to be numbered. Once he's gone, there won't be anyone left to hold our leash. That's when you and me are done with all this, but only then."

"You got it all figured out. Like they're just gonna show up and arrest Mr. Woodson and pretend everyone working for him—including you and me—are just innocent victims."

"We won't be around for them to find us. I guarantee it."

"Just don't be surprised when all this blows up in your face," said Sam. "You can't run away and play hero, it's one or the other."

That last sentence stuck in Rob's head. He'd never thought of himself as a hero, in fact, he was more than sure he'd become the opposite of that recently. He knew good and well the plan was to run, but he had no intention of playing the hero in all this. Of course, considering the fact that they were headed to Mr. Woodson's place to track down where those children escaped from and see if they could find anything they could use in their fight against that man.

THEIR DRIVE TOOK MORE than an hour before anything looked familiar. It gave Rob more time than he wanted to ponder what Sam had told him and whether or not he could live up to such a lofty title. He might never admit it, but it kind of felt good to think of himself in such a light, rather than the indebted thief unable to escape the consequences of his own actions.

The truck came to a stop at the end of a dirt road, lost in a maze of woods. Rob had been there before, and it brought back only painful memories. Watching people he had worked so closely with, people he could even see himself coming to respect, get gunned down so violently, all for the already-fattened wallet of Mr. Woodson, made him feel a swirl of rage in his gut. It took a hard blink and a deep breath to get his wits about him. Cool night air dried his throat, and the swishing of limbs and leaves around him calmed his nerves. An occasional, brief few-seconds song of a Northern Mockingbird broke up the nighttime tension as Rob and Sam both eased their way into the woods.

Rob held his hand above the .357 strapped to his hip. The walnut grip was cold to the touch, and the grain rubbed against his fingers every so often as he walked. It was centimeters away from his grasp, and milliseconds away from spewing the flames of hell from its barrel, taking the lift of anything standing in its way, leaving behind only a smoking brass casing in its wake. For now, it rested in the cracked and worn leather holster, patient as it always was.

He and Sam didn't need to say a word about what was about to happen. They'd already talked about everything. As much as they wanted to free any other children locked away wherever Mr. Woodson had them, they were seeking vindication for themselves through undeniable proof of his wrongdoings. Rob glanced over his shoulder at Sam, who was walking identically to him, with one hand hovering over a pistol tucked at his waistband.

They passed the bunkhouse building that they'd stayed in not too long ago before the incident at the Coleman Ranch, and found their way through a tree line in the distance not too long after. They weren't sure where they were going, but they knew where the children had come from. Their best bet was to just follow their tracks and see where it took them. After a half hour of trudging through brush too thick for any reasonable person to walk through, Sam finally questioned their method.

"What happens if we don't find anything?"

Rob thought about his answer for just a few seconds. "Then we look over our shoulders a little more when we do make our run for it."

"Fair enough."

Their hike dragged on for another hour before something worth finding started to make itself known. It started as a shadow in the night, darker than the blackened sky, starless and eager to hide the moon. At first, Rob wondered if it was a cluster of trees at first, but as he crept closer, the shadow took shape as a warehouse covered in rusted tin and surrounded by woods in every direction. To most, it would have been a hay barn or some old man's shop, but Rob knew immediately there was something else inside. The feeling hit him in the gut like a strike from a drunk man who just lost a bet with the man eyeballing his wife.

"There it is," he whispered to Sam.

"Who's going first?"

"I thought you were."

"I thought *you* were. This was your idea."

Rob sighed. He was right. This was his problem to deal with, and he was lucky to have Sam at his side. If they lived long enough to see their freedom, he even thought he might call that man a friend one day. For now, they were just two disgruntled employees, and they were ready to burn the place down on their way out.

Rob took a step forward, allowing his fingers to curl around the handle of the revolver at his hip. The warehouse was taller than he first thought. I t seemed impossible to construct such a place in the middle of nowhere, without taking down any trees or building a road that connects it to anything worth driving on. When he grabbed the metal latch to drag the front door open, he gave a passing thought to whether or not he should have found a less conspicuous way in. But when nothing happened with the door wide open, he took it upon himself to walk right on in.

Sam was right behind him, entering the warehouse, void of any lighting, like a black hole swallowing them up in the night. Rob went ahead and lifted the revolver out of his holster and pushed his other hand to the handle, keeping the firearm close to his chest just in case. They weren't sure what they would find inside, but they knew they had to get their hands on something— just in case Mr. Woodson had paid off the right people at the right time. They couldn't take any chances.

They wouldn't find any evidence inside the building. There were no lost children or women chained to headboards, no pallets of drugs sealed from the noses of dogs, or stacks of cash lying around waiting to be injected into a legal company. There weren't any important folders or computers to find the smoking gun they conspired to discover. There wasn't even so much as a footprint left behind of those who hauled everything out at the last minute. It was empty and silent and dark.

"Well, this was a waste of—"

BOOM.

An explosion of gunfire cried out around them, illuminating the warehouse with muzzle blast flames, shrouding it even more with the smoke that followed soon after. There were bullets coming from all around Rob and Sam, and they had nothing left to do but dance in the flickering shadows of death before scrambling for cover.

Bam. Bam. Bam.

"Where the hell are they?" Rob shouted to Sam despite only being inches apart.

"Just shoot!"

Rob looked frantically in every direction. He was lost in the onslaught of gunfire raining down like a circle of hell he wanted no part of. He held too few bullets, hid behind cover too weak to remain useful, to ever have a hope of fighting his way out of it. Rob had spent his days riding and sorting, not running and shooting. When he looked back at Sam, he saw a man who wasn't bothered by any of that.

Sam had already almost emptied the cylinder of his own revolver. He yanked the trigger out of pure adrenaline, barely looking at where he was shooting, but doing a heck of a lot better at fighting back than Rob was. When one of the men let out a pained grunt before a familiar *thud* hit the floor, Rob knew Sam had actually tagged one of the gunmen.

For the first time since they'd ducked behind a pile of haphazardly stacked metal building materials, including studs, joists, siding, and screws, Rob had an inkling of hope that he might live to see the sun creep over the horizon in the morning. It was just enough to convince him to join the fight and squeeze the trigger.

Breaking from cover to find the closest muzzle blast in the pitch black shadows between gunshots, shooting where the blast had been, and hoping a bullet would strike a gunman, became something like a game of life-and-death for Rob and Sam. They rocked back and forth on their heels, trying to maintain cover, extending one arm out with the revolver clutched in their fist to shoot a stream of fire and smoke with every round. This went on for longer than most likely anyone in that warehouse wanted it to.

Rob fell flat on his ass behind the stack of steel and popped the cylinder out of his revolver. The screaming hot brass fell one by one onto the concrete floor, bouncing and rolling away as Rob jammed round after round back into the cylinder to get back into the action. He used his offhand to lock it back into place and fumbled for the hammer as quickly as his thumb would allow. When it slammed forward and another bullet fired out from the end of the bluing barrel in the night, Rob knew it was time to try something else.

"Let's get 'em!" he shouted, while already running away from the cover that had kept them alive so far.

"What the—"

Rob was already making his way up the steel staircase, his boots pounding the metal, clanking and rattling everything that could make a sound during his climb. He hoped Sam would take his lead and go for the other staircase on the other side of the warehouse, but he didn't get that lucky. While Sam fired from down below, Rob did the hard part and faced down the siren calls of death and charged ahead. He couldn't see what he was running toward, and he was just waiting for the stinging, burning, paralyzing pain of a bullet shredding through his body, but it never came.

He finally made out a silhouette of a man just ahead, who was kneeling down and trying to reload his own gun. Rob didn't hesitate, and he showed the same mercy that the faceless gunman had shown him when he entered the building. He raised his arm and aimed the .357 at the man's chest and squeezed the trigger. Stopping power mixed with traumatic surprise sent the man sprawling backward, dead in an instant, but it also drew the attention of every other gunman he'd come to the fight alongside.

They wanted revenge for another fallen one of their own, and they opened fire, all aimed right at his position. Rob kept moving, though. As Sam cleared a path with cover fire from just beneath where Rob was walking, the fight didn't actually start to turn in their favor until an undoubtedly lucky round fired from Sam pierced the gut of a man who exposed himself at the wrong time.

Rob didn't know how many of them were left, but he knew there wasn't much that could stand in his way at this point, so he pressed on. The hammer clicked back and slammed forward five more times before Rob was forced to duck behind a wooden crate to reload from the loose rounds in his pocket. He fumbled for just a few seconds, trying to grasp the hollow-point bullets from his pockets and drop them into the cylinder. Bullets whistled by, inches from his head, while others slammed into the wooden crate, sending thousands of splinters into the air.

The cover he'd found afforded him just a few seconds to glance around the inside of the warehouse, locked in a firefight. His eyes had adjusted to the darkness, and he could just barely make out the two staircases on either side of the building connected by an overhang walkway that crossed the center of the building. That's where he was standing. He just so happened to notice the doorway leading out of the warehouse at the bottom of the other set of stairs, and an idea he never wanted to have popped into his head.

The next thing he knew, his boots were pounding the expanded metal floors, and his trigger finger was squeezing the trigger over and over again at anything unfortunate enough to move in his line of sight. He wasn't the only one making a run for it, though. Just as he came to the corner of the walkway, a man blocked his path forward, dressed in a jacket too heavy for the humid weather and a crooked mask just barely covering his face. To Rob's surprise, he dropped the pistol in his right hand, screamed something only he could understand, and turned to run for his life down the same staircase Rob was running toward. For longer than Rob would ever admit to another living soul, he considered what kind of man he would be if he shot another man in the back while he was doing the very same thing—fleeing. It was an unimaginable depth to sink to, but Rob found himself questioning if it was a place he'd be willing to go.

Rob's gun fell to his side, and he turned his head before he changed his mind.

Sam was locked in an endless fight against two gunmen who had him right in their sights. The exchange of gunpowder, flame, and lead could only last so long. Rob heard the door he wanted so desperately to leave through, slam shut, then watched as Sam locked eyes with his. There wasn't fear or surrender in his stare, it was a dare, challenging Rob to come to terms with whether he'd save his own life by abandoning the fight, or risk it by drawing all the attention to himself.

This time, it wasn't even a question in his mind. Rob was already running. The door had failed to latch shut, offering him the perfect chance to shove his way forward and leave the fight behind. Moonlight coaxed him through, urging him to escape, to live, only so that he could continue to run for just one more day.

What he saw first came to his surprise, enough to stop him in his tracks. There was the man who'd just run from him. His mask was shoved into his face, planted firmly in the dirt. Rob wasn't sure if he was dead, but the way he was lying on his stomach sure didn't look promising. By the time the thought occurred to him that someone must have done this to the poor guy, it was too late to see the strike coming.

Rob crumpled to the ground, and his head jerked back even harder, colliding against the backside rusted steel of the warehouse. His vision was black and blurry. He was disoriented from the fall and struggling to breathe. There was a throbbing, dull ache on the right side of his head. He felt consciousness slipping away while his limbs refused to move even a single muscle. A soft grunt escaped his mouth, followed by a strand of saliva, creeping down his chin.

Rob's only vivid thought was hoping that the drool wasn't blood before a familiar voice came from on top of him. He couldn't see a face, or even a silhouette, in the dazed vision fading further away every second. At first, the words came slowly and from a million miles away, like someone shouting threats from inside a passing vehicle on the highway.

"I thought for sure you'd be the first one to run away," the voice came in and out. "I guess even cowards like you can still surprise me."

A name he wished he could forget, came to Rob's mind just before he succumbed to the darkness taking over him and drifted to a sleep he wanted no part of— O'Kelley.

Chapter 20

"I'm telling you. Mr. Woodson *hates* his guts. I'm surprised he didn't kill the guy himself, honestly."

"I will not condone you killing a man."

"If I don't, someone else will, and we won't get anything out of it. He's on his last leg already, so it's just a matter of time. Trust me."

"I don't care. If you kill that man, there will come a day where I'll take a seat on a podium in front of a bunch of people all too eager to cast judgment, and I'll have to explain how that man's life was worth whatever we are putting in front of them. I'll tell them how there was no other way, how, without his sacrifice, such terrible evil could not have been kept at bay. I'm here to tell you beyond a shadow of a doubt—it won't matter. Not a single word of it. I'll have used the state to gun a man down without due process, and they'll never believe a word I say."

"You trying to tell me this call is being recorded?"

"Your type really doesn't have a clue about principles."

"You want me to get in deeper with these people? This is how it works. I'll gain respect. I'll take his job. I'll earn favor. It will put me in the know for all that kind of shit you like to keep askin' me about. You're the one always saying I don't tell you enough, well, I'm here to tell you, this is what it's gonna take."

"And what's that, exactly?"

"I'm gonna kill ol' Robbie Ford."

As resolute as Sheriff Tom T. Turpin was, as much as he liked to think of himself as a steadfast man of honor, integrity, and moral sensibility—the kind most believed was lost to history decades ago—he thought about just how helpful that man's death might be. It would get Sam's foot in the door, sure, but it would also wrap up his own dealings with Rob in a nice bow that no other authorities would ever be able to sniff out.

It should've been an easy decision. The badge pinned on his chest meant the answer wasn't a decision at all, actually. Tom was meant to take O'Kelley in, put him in cuffs, then go do the same damn thing to Dalton Woodson and anyone unlucky enough to be around him at the time. It wasn't an easy decision, though. The years had grinded him down and chipped away at his own spine. Even if he knew the words to tell others about his beliefs, following them so strictly at every corner was harder now than ever before. Deep down, he knew that meant only one thing—it was time to retire.

"No, you ain't," he said finally, offering a gentle, heartwarming boost to his own ego. "You kill him, and I will fry your ass in a chair myself."

"It's already happening, old man," said O'Kelley. "I shouldn't have even told you, but you can't stop it now. I can guarantee that. Bossman is gonna say my name next, and we're both gonna be better off for it. You'll see. Next time you hear from me, you'll be wondering how that ratty county jail of yours got filled up a dozen times over with enough cartel assholes to put the entire drug industry out of business."

"Hold on," Tom said.

"Not yet, Sheriff. I had one more thing to tell—"

He pushed the phone back onto the receiver and watched the button labeled, *Line 1*, blink red over and over again. Tom didn't care what else O'Kelley had to say at this point. His door had opened, and Denise was leaning halfway into his office with her hand still gripped onto the doorknob. Her beaming smile took the edge off just a little, and in the middle of everything Tom was going through, he decided to think about what he'd say if he was twenty years younger, hell, even ten years younger. These days, he just didn't have much in him than the usual response.

"What?" he asked, dry as he always had.

"There are a couple of suits here, say they're looking for you," Denise said, her expression turning to worry as she spoke. "Are you out of the office right now? Maybe they should check back later?" She asked with a hint in her tone and a glint in her eyes.

"No," Tom said, with the same reluctance that kept him from wishing death on that criminal Robbie. "Just send 'em in, let's get this over with."

Denise took a step inside and closed the door. This was unlike her. Rob watched her face turn upside down with worry as she searched for words that would not come. It was a few awkward seconds before her eyes started to water and her lips began to quiver. Her cheeks were flushed, and her posture was weaker than

Tom had ever seen. When a single tear streamed down her cheek, staining the makeup on her face with a reflection of the fluorescent lighting, she finally said what was on her mind.

"This might be the last time I see you, Tom," she spat out, attempting not to sob in the middle of her words.

"Why the hell would you say that?"

"I ain't never seen suits like that," she said. "And they look so pissed off. They look like you just before we get a new long-term resident at the jailhouse."

"That don't mean nothing."

"I been here long enough to know something ain't right. If you don't want to tell me what's goin' on, that's on you. But just so you know, that means I don't have to listen to you. If I can keep them away for just a little longer, maybe this case will finally bust open and they'll come back to thank you. They'd be stupid not to!"

"Denise," Tom started. "I sure appreciate everything you do for me. Always have. I probably haven't told you enough. Hell, who knows, maybe in another lifetime…" Tom started to think differently about what he was getting ready to say. "Look, what I can tell you is that District Judge Coleman has had enough of everything that's been going on. He said a couple of people were going to come take this thing off my hands, but I think maybe he had different ideas."

"Like what?"

"I don't know what he knows, but it's gotta be bad if he sent people to take me out of the game," Tom said, as he plucked the straw cowboy hat from its usual resting place on the corner of his desk and pushed it down on his head. "And who knows, maybe they really are here to help. Only one way to find out."

Denise finally let her head sink and did her best to stop the tears from flowing. She looked up at him with reddened eyes and nodded her head.

They had wasted too much time during their back and forth. A muscle-bound man clad in a black suit and matching tie pushed his way past Denise and forced himself into the office before she even had a chance to wipe the last tear from her face. Just behind the first suit was the second one, this time, it was a woman with a tightly held ponytail, revealing a stern face and scrunched eyebrows. Tom knew what was behind her eyes, and right then, he knew he may as well start saying his prayers, because his time as sheriff had most likely come to a bittersweet end.

"Sheriff, I assume?" the meathead said.

"The one and only."

"You've had a good run."

"I ain't done yet, either."

"You are now," the woman finally interjected.

"What are they talking about, Tom? They can't be here!" Denise shouted. "What are they talking about?"

"Ma'am," the woman turned to face Denise. "Save it."

"No!" Denise shot back. "You can't be in here!"

"It's all right, Denise," said Tom, before turning his attention back to the two suits. "Right when you two walked through my front door, lookin' like you just walked out of the backroom of some fancy bar in New York City, I had a single question pop into my head that I just can't help but ask before we get too far into all this."

Both of the two suits stood there looking at him,

blank expressions plastered across their face like they hadn't had an honest word spoken to them since they left their parents' home. It wasn't in their nature to do anything other than what someone above their pay grade told them to do. The sheriff's question hadn't struck a nerve yet to pull them out of their professional trance, but it was sure about to.

"Whose payroll are you on?"

A few minutes ago, Tom wished he had been ten years younger for reasons entirely different than what he was feeling now. But as the two suits moved across his office quicker than he could move if he tried his damndest, he wished he was at least thirty years younger. At this point in life, he'd be lucky to get by one, but he knew he wouldn't stand a chance now. Back in his prime, he could've taken them both on and laughed while he did it.

They say your life flashes before your eyes when you're about to die. Considering his life was pretty much coming to an end, Tom thought for sure there would be a litany of memories he wanted to run away from rushing back to his head, but that just wasn't the case. The only thing he thought of when they rushed at him were the looks in the eyes of the people trapped behind bars in that warehouse. The people he'd turned away from, their pain and suffering, their wishes for freedom and family, their dread and anguish, hope and resilience—it was all the cost they would have to pay for his own decisions.

Because of that, Tom didn't even rise from his squeaking leather chair. He just let what was due come his way. False promises had led him to become the very thing he was meant to lock away from society. He knew his time was coming, and like most, he always thought he had just a little more time, but he knew it was only right if he only ever saw the free world through a window and bars too small to fit through.

The meathead was rougher than he needed to be. Tom felt the back of his hair start to pull for a split second before his face slammed into the desk, almost hard enough to break his nose. Denise screamed at the top of her lungs, and he grunted hard enough to lose his breath, the sounds mixing into the clatter of everything on his desk hitting the floor.

"We know what you've been doing," the woman said as she pulled cuffs out from behind her back.

"We know who you've been working with."

"It all ends now."

Tom couldn't lift his head up from the desk. The meathead's calloused hand was too strong for him to budge. That didn't stop him from being able to speak, though.

"You don't know shit," he said. "Trust me."

"Let me ask you something," the woman said as she tightened the cuffs around the sheriff's wrists more than she ever should have. "How many men do you know who like to talk too much?"

Tom thought about it for all of two seconds before a face and a name came to mind—O'Kelley. Before the woman could speak again, he thought about what that son of a bitch had to say before he'd hung the phone up on him just a few minutes ago.

"Now that we've got that out of the way," said the meathead, "I want you to think long and hard about everything you ever told that man. Because that is what we know. Everything."

"Then you know there ain't much time left," Tom

said as the woman lifted his face off the desk. "I'm almost there."

"You're done."

"Simple as that."

The woman reached up and wrapped her cold fingers around the star pinned on the sheriff's chest. She twisted and yanked the star until it tore through his shirt and left him as nothing but a shell of a man.

"You shouldn't have taken a deal with those people. The cartel isn't to be fucked with."

"The cartel?" Denise shouted between her sobs.

"You don't listen to anything they say," said Tom. "It's that damn district judge. He's been after me for years. He ain't gonna get me, though!" The sheriff was spitting mad, his face red and his words laced with the kind of rage that only comes from being backed in a corner. He shifted his gaze from one suit to the next as his fury poured out. "He ain't gonna put me away for a damned thing! I'll be back! This county needs me more than any of you know!"

The suits had Sheriff Tom by each of the shoulders when they started to drag him. His flailing legs and swinging fists didn't hurt anybody, but given the chance, he would've beaten both of the suits senseless if it meant he could work one more day behind that star. It was all he cared about, all he knew.

There are some men in the world who do everything for their family, live and die, and pass on whatever they built in life to their children. Those are the people who find the meaning of legacy in their last days, or at the very least, discover its truest meaning. Then, there are some men who only know work, who know only the struggle and sweat and aches that come with a hard day. They don't have time for family, or for themselves. All of their time has been traded away before it comes to pass.

Sheriff thought he'd been the latter for damn near all his life. He thought the work was all that mattered, that chasing justice and putting in the hours was the point of waking up every morning. As he was kicking and screaming and fighting, the world turned against him, he couldn't help but be beside himself, letting his thoughts dwell on the life he'd turned his back on. A family would be nice to have about now. Someone who cared about him, not what he could do for them. He'd chased justice for years and years and years, and it led him to the hands of those doing the very same thing. Somewhere along the way, he'd lost himself, not just to a deal with Dalton D. Woodson or the criminal under-belly he called home, but to the blasphemous idea that he could make a difference in the world.

The world has always been the same to people like him, and there isn't anything or anyone that could ever change it.

Chapter 21

It was dust that woke him, pelting his dry and cracked lips, covering his face, and finding its way into his closed eyes.

Rob couldn't move. His hands wouldn't budge, nor his feet. His legs were locked away from his own mind, and his arms had been above his head so long, there was no blood in either of them. Something scratched his wrists, tore at his skin, and threatened to draw blood if he wiggled too much. It was the same pain he felt on his ankles. Before he was conscious of what he should be doing, he did the only thing that came natural—he tried to break free of his bonds.

"Shit!" His voice was rough and harsh, and the pain damn near sent him back into unconsciousness.

It wasn't leather or rope keeping him from moving his limbs, restricting even the slightest movement—it was razor sharp 4-point barbed wire. He'd felt those cuts before more than a few times in his life. As the blood started to trickle down his forearm, panic began to rise from the pit of his belly. He wiggled and strained against the barbed wire sinking itself into his skin until the panic worked its way up through his chest and became lodged in his throat.

Before he could even think about what might have happened to him, he was a bloody mess from his failed attempts at escaping. His breath was ragged, and his eyes burned with dirt and tears. He couldn't see anything through a blindfold tied around his head, but he could feel the awkward position he was forced to lie in. His hands were raised above his head, as if he was hoisted by them. His shoulders carried the weight of what felt like his entire body, and he could only feel the ground from his waist down.

Just when he thought his situation couldn't get any worse, he heard an unfortunately familiar whinny. That's when everything fell into place. He'd been tied up to the back of a horse, belly down, and he was about to get dragged just like Lee Van Cleef was in *Death Rides a Horse.* There was nothing he could do to prepare for what was about to happen. As much as he dreaded the coming pain from the rocks and sticks tearing into his stomach, it was the barbed wire around his wrists and ankles that sent him into a furious frenzy. He thrashed and kicked and screamed with everything he had, but it only made matters worse. The barbed wire seemed to twist and tighten against what was left of the skin it had pierced into.

"You just couldn't leave well enough alone," a voice came from above his head. It was deep and raspy, as if to hide their true voice. "You can't run, now."

"I'll kill you, you son of a bitch!"

Hollow threats were all Rob could conjure at this point. He had no chance of escaping, but he could damn sure make life hell for whoever it was that put him in this situation. With his hands and feet already going numb from the restraints, he felt more empowered to thrash around behind the horse standing just in front of him. He barrel-rolled and pushed off the ground until he couldn't breathe anymore, and his body was forced to go limp.

"You all done?" the voice came again.

It was a man's voice, that was all Rob could be sure of. He couldn't recognize who it belonged to, and he had no clue why he was being targeted. All he could assume was his life sins had finally caught up to him. He'd always imagined it would be sirens and handcuffs, though, not frontier justice.

There was a quick *click-click* that came from the rider no more than a few feet in front of him before his worst fears came to realization. His stomach was on fire within seconds as it scraped against the ground and peeled the flesh from where it was supposed to be. He could feel the blood start to pour out from his wounds, and still, there was nothing he could do.

It started slow at first. Then, they went a little faster, bit by bit, until the horse had settled into a deadly trot that left Rob paralyzed in pain. His helpless body was a ragdoll behind the horse. All he could do was use what little strength he had to keep his back arched and his stomach off the ground, taking the brunt force onto his knees and shins, but that didn't last long. He had no strength to give.

He was dragged in silence for what felt like hours, even though it had only been minutes, before he came to a creeping pace. The horse walked as if there were toddlers on its back at a circus, but it was just enough for Rob to feel every pebble and hole in the ground as he was pulled around and around.

"Please!" he shouted before thinking. It came instinctively, but he refused to be the person who died begging for an end that fate did not have in store. "If you don't stop, this will be the last goddam thing you ever do!"

Another hollow threat. It did nothing but make his situation worse, too. The horse started to pick up speed, and Rob started hollering just about every cuss word he'd ever heard in his life to whoever was close enough to hear him. This time, he was able to muster just enough strength to roll over onto his back and let his bare stomach, bloodied and bruised and scraped, face the gentle warmth of the sunlight and cool breeze wicking away the burning sensation for even just a few seconds.

They were at a trot again when a bumpy, rough patch of ground sent Rob higher into the air than he could control. He landed on his stomach again with a guttural grunt, forcing the air out of his lungs and leaving him on the verge of losing consciousness. He was slipping, as much as he didn't want to, and he was embarrassed by the thoughts that started to come to his head. He was used to the urge to run away, but the urge to give up, to stop fighting, and to let this stranger keep dragging him until there was nothing left to drag, wasn't something he'd ever come to terms with before. He knew he had to fight it, but there was nothing left in him to summon. This wasn't a classic Western where the white hat finds the courage to do the right thing and everything just miraculously falls into place to take down the black hat. He was tied to the backside of a horse with barbed wire, and he wouldn't ever walk away unless something, or someone, let him. That was a simple fact.

After going in circles for longer than he could keep track of, Rob had decided on being stubborn until the last breath escaped his lips. If there was one constant truth he had long abided by, it was a rather simple desire, and that was to not die. He'd been a coward since he was born and that meant he was all too willing to run for his life. If pure stubbornness would be the only way to keep running from the shadows of death itself, then so be it.

When left turns had proven to only drive him to madness, in a haze of torturous pain and misery and exhaustion, the circles came to a stop. The barbed wire around his wrists shifted, and he grunted as his head fell limp. They were easing to a stop again, but this time there were no words to mutter or empty threats to spew. There was only a faint trace of oxygen to be found in Rob's lungs, and he could not spare any for the man who'd put him through the agony he'd endured.

Rocks and dirt turned to grass, and he found a new way to be thankful in life, one that he never hoped to experience again. Aside from the occasional pinecone, the change in terrain was more than he could've asked for. Everything burned. He could barely breathe. The barbed wire still held his wrist and ankles tight as he hung from the end of a saddle. They eventually slowed to a stop, and Rob finally gave up on any concept of time. He didn't know if he laid there on his belly, still suspended by his wrists, for a minute or an hour, but that too would eventually come to a much welcome end.

With a sudden snip, the barbed wire lost tension and he face planted into the dirt. He listened to the hooves of a horse gently walking away from him. He may have been a fool for hoping it was coming to an end, but he allowed it anyway while he laid there in the silent darkness. When the ants started to crawl onto him and the cool breeze of the evening swept in, there was finally a commotion that wasn't his own cries.

A heavy boot planted right next to his ear, and he felt someone at his ankles, fidgeting with the barbed wire, doing no favors to keep it away from digging into his skin and sending dreams of blood down into the dirt. The blood had dried, and it hurt enough to pry what little tears Rob could muster out of his eyes. He'd never felt such horrid pain before. This time, he found himself practically begging to have whoever stood beside him pull the barbed wire from his wrists. There was no such luck, though.

With his feet free, the only thing he could manage to do with any motivation was to curl up as much as his wrecked stomach would allow. The fetal position was the only thing that helped. If he could have stood up and sprinted away from it all, he would've in an instant, but he just didn't have it in him. For now, all he could do was fight the tears back and do his best to keep breathing.

A pair of roughened hands grabbed him by the shoulder harder than he thought a man could, dragged him no more than ten feet, and propped him up against what had to be a T-post. It dug into his back and forced him to hunch over, putting his stomach in even more unbearable pain. He grunted in response, but that was all he could manage.

"You never stood a chance," a voice finally came, familiar this time, and sending Rob into an immediate fury.

"I fuckin' *knew* it was you, O'Kelly! You did this to

me? I'm gonna bury your ass shallow as soon as I get the chance. I swear to God!"

"You didn't know shit. Stop lyin' to yourself."

"Did you kill Sam?"

"You might want to worry about yourself for a little bit, buddy."

"You ain't gonna do nothin'," Rob said and spat without knowing where to look. "I know who you are."

It wasn't half a second after he finished the last word when Rob felt O'Kelley lean in closer than he ever should have. His stench filled Rob's nostrils and made him turn up his lip in disgust.

"I know who *you* are, too," O'Kelley whispered. "You coward."

Rob moved fast. He kicked with both of his feet, hoping his boots would land hard enough to give him just a second-long advantage. He thrashed out, scrambled to get on his side in the process, trying to get himself upright to make a run for it.

The blow he took to the stomach before he ever got to his feet was almost more than he could take. O'Kelley's own square-toe leather boot hit him right in the belly, his torn and bloodied flesh screamed with searing pain, and all Rob could do was yelp and cry and roll in the dirt.

"I tried to tell the sheriff this had to happen," O'Kelley talked nonchalantly, as if he didn't see Rob writhing around. "You are a tough one to wrangle, I'll give you that. Dalton likes to think that makes you useful, and yes, we are on a first-name basis, just in case you were wondering. Anyways, he says we all have our role to play, that you've brought in a lot of money for him and that's hard to replace. Can you believe that?"

Rob was back to only grunting. He still hadn't even caught his breath, and he damn sure couldn't find any to spare a few cuss words at O'Kelley. The words came and went, no different than the breeze across his face and the song of grasshoppers and cicadas rising and falling in the distance. He couldn't tell if it was sweat or blood dripping down his face, but his eyes never did stop burning, so it didn't make much of a difference either way.

"If we all have a role to play and your only value is how much money you can bring Bossman clutched in your bloody fist, I hate to tell you," O'Kelley continued, "I'm gonna win that fight."

"You don't get it," Rub muttered. "I didn't either when I first started." He was still lying on his side in the dirt, unable to bring himself to move on his own. "We don't ever come out on top. We don't win. The criminals and cartels are the only ones who win. We are a supplier, and Bossman is the dealer."

"No," said O'Kelley. "You don't get it. This is how the world works. Always has been. Those men are just getting what's theirs. Same as me. Doesn't really matter how, does it?"

"I guess not."

"So, you understand why I gotta, you know," O'Kelley said, leaving Rob to conclude his gist was most likely referring to his own death since he couldn't see O'Kelley's fingers in the shape of a gun and pointed at his own forehead. "I just can't do it yet. I need Dalton to see it, to witness exactly what I can bring to the table. It ain't only your head on the line."

Rob turned his head, trying to loosen the blindfold just a little, but to no avail. He wiggled himself back upright, hoping for what little support the T-post provided that he'd taken for granted.

"You see, that idea of yours to steal from the sale barn and dump off to Dalton was pretty clever. Sure, you didn't consider the EID tag problem, how there were dozens of different ranches contributing to that thousand head you boosted. You know what kind of logistics went into registering them to all those aliases? Probably not. Why would you? Let me tell you, they're still tryin' to fix all those tattoos on their ears, and that crew is cussin' our name. And for good reason, being completely honest."

"That shit ain't my fault," said Rob, finally finding his balance against the T-post and trying to ignore the barbed wire still digging into his wrists. "Tags and tattoos were never my problem. I gave Bossman more cattle than he could handle. We were makin' money. He knows that. Maybe you don't?"

"You really ain't in a position to be talking like that," said O'Kelley.

Before Rob knew it, those same calloused fingers that grabbed his shoulders moments ago gripped the blindfold wrapped around his head and yanked it off, taking hair and skin with it as he pulled. Rob jerked back, trying to let his eyes adjust to the air despite the burning and watering that seemed to never come to an end.

At first, there was nothing to see but blurry darkness as far as his eyes would take him. As the seconds ticked by, a gangly silhouette of a man wearing a cowboy hat tipped too far up to be taken seriously. Rob could just barely make out a soft red glow of a cigarette in his hand, and for a moment, he realized he thought about the fact that O'Kelley had never smoked around him before. It was admittedly an insignificant detail about the man he'd rustled with, but it came to Rob as an admission—he didn't have a clue who O'Kelley really was.

"The only thing you can do now is lay there and wait for me to drag Dalton over here so he can watch me put an end to all this for good."

"The law will come knocking, one way or another," said Rob. "You already set that in motion."

"You don't remember? That was *you* talkin' to the sheriff. You're the one who got the law comin' down on us."

Stabbed in the back again. It was something Rob had long gotten used to. It was a consequence of always running, and he knew that as well as anyone. All anyone ever saw of him was his back as he hauled ass in the opposite direction. More times than not, this was where he ended up.

His eyesight had finally started to return as O'Kelley continued to lecture him like a gun hand holding up a bank with a grudge against the whole town. He couldn't stop talking, but all Rob could focus on were the trees surrounding them in every direction. They looked familiar, like he'd been there a lifetime ago. It was hazy, but the fear he felt in his belly told him he wasn't wrong.

"Now, you'll be right here when we get back," said O'Kelley before kneeling down in front of Rob. "You're gonna hear all manner of things comin' through the trees, just over yonder," he said, motioning with his hand south of where they were. "To get rid of all that trouble you dumped on Dalton's doorstep, we got the biggest spenders south of the border to come clean house. They're buyin' up all the women and children, the heroin, fentanyl, and methamphetamine, and even the explosives, everything down to the last computer. You ain't gonna see a dime out of it, but think of it this way…"

Rob let his head hang at last. He didn't care about the barbed wire digging into him or the blood running from his stomach beneath torn clothing and flesh. He didn't care about the money or the coming sunrise he may never see. He just wanted to burn it all down and leave it all behind him.

"The largest narco cattle ranchin' operation this side of the border is gonna be built right on top of your grave. Ain't that something to be proud of?"

Chapter 22

"I see a lot of familiar faces tonight. Hay más caras que conozco que no conozco."

"You may think we are hiding in the shadows, or you might even think we are exposed out in the open, for all the world to see. Te equivocas. No hay nada que pueda detener lo que estamos haciendo. Así es como funciona el mundo ahora."

"If you have never been here before or if you just want to browse our wares, here is how things are going to go. Necesitas tener tu cartera lista. We have pairs and bred heifers, butcher steers, and yearlings. If you were lookin' for bulls, you're at the wrong sale, check back in the spring. ¿Qué significa esto para ti? Aquí está lo que vas a comprar. Pairs are for you older gentlemen, and the bred heifers are for the younger men out there. Butcher steers come in all types and sizes, from tech to guns, and even though we only have a handful of yearlings, those are for the big spenders with deep pockets. We have dozens of lots available tonight, so break out those untraceable offshore checks, and gastemos dinero para apoyar una buena causa."

"My campaign for the United States Congress begins tonight. Starting with lot number one, a fine specimen of a female, a black Angus-bred heifer. You can see the pictures to my right and the video of her to my left. Let's start the bidding at ten thousand."

Rob listened to the worst of what this world has to offer, spend their fortunes on pure evil incarnate. Their horrors would be hidden by the towering pines and carried away from history itself by the wind blowing through the limbs. He listened to what he helped to create, and what would surely become his dying legacy if he wasn't able to find a way out. He'd be blamed for the worst of it, and in a way, those people wouldn't be wrong, as he had a role to play.

"Sold! Two hundred and fifty *thousand* dollars! She's got a mighty fine home to go to, that's for sure."

Bossman's voice was indistinguishable. It echoed through the night like a phantom, haunting Rob's every thought. He carried on, booming with pride at the cash being laundered through his stolen cattle to purchase what couldn't be found in the open market. It was a ranch in name only, where its real purpose lay in the transactional nature of man and beast, blurring the lines between the two with more money than most ever wanted to believe was possible.

Rob was hunched over against the same T-post, struggling to breathe from the wounds on his stomach and still trying to wrap his mind around what had happened. The rustlers were roped into their work due to their own decisions. Rob was no different than the rest. Their backgrounds and upbringings, their life choices all culminated in the law chasing them down, leaving no other options but to take a deal with the devil for a final chance at freedom. They were all men forced to play the hands they were dealt, but O'Kelley turned out to be the kind of man who'd only play the hand he could sneak up his sleeve. Most just wanted to pay off their debt to Mr. Woodson, but not O'Kelley. That was a man ready to do anything it took to climb the ranks of the criminal underbelly, and there wasn't a cattle rustler, cartel leader, or law enforcement agency that would stand in his way.

For Rob, the chips had already fallen. At this point, even though it was more painful than he could imagine, he was surprised he could still draw breath. The people he'd surrounded himself with did what they do best—used him and left him for dead, all alone in the middle of nowhere. He shouldn't have expected anything less, but even he would have to admit, getting dragged by a horse like it was the Wild West was nothing like he could have ever dreamed of.

He had nothing left to ante up with, and everyone knew that, but what they didn't know about was that phone call he had with the sheriff. Whether anything would come out of it was yet to be seen, but even Rob couldn't help but let out a chuckle at the thought of their party in the woods being crashed like a bunch of underage teenagers with more alcohol than they could hide.

He winced at the pain that came with laughing, then tried to adjust himself on the T-post. When he leaned up, he felt something lodged in his right ass cheek, and the adrenaline that coursed through his veins in just a few seconds damn near sent him into shock. He scrambled in the dirt, kicking his legs and trying to get his hands bound by barbed wire to his back pocket with fingers soaked in blood. It was a desperate act, but if his suspicions were true, he could bring himself to believe that his life hadn't been completely forfeit just yet.

In the mad rush to get his hands in his back pocket, the small, black leather journal fell into the dirt with a *thud* that sent shivers down Rob's spine. He couldn't believe it had stayed with him through the torturing he'd endured, but there it was, lying inconspicuously in the earth, begging Rob to find his future in the words of a dead man one more time. The feeling of the journal in his hands again was no different than drops of cool water to a man on the brink of death in the desert. It was hope incarnate resting in his hands, forged by a man who bore the title of a coward long before he'd ever come to know his hateful ways.

His fingers stained every page black and red. It was almost impossible to hold the journal with 4-point barbed wire sunk into his flesh and muscle and dried blood. He struggled through the pain regardless. He was growing dizzy from blood loss, through drowsy eyes and an attention span broken by jolts of pain shooting through his entire body, he tried to focus on words he could barely read. Black ink on paper wasting away to time itself was even harder to read in the middle of a night filled with only clouds blocking the guidance of the moon and stars.

He skimmed over the death of Robert Ford's horse, the towns they raided, and the banks they robbed. He remembered all too well their life on the run. He stopped reading when he saw the entry that led to Robert's most infamous decision, the one that led him to strike his own deal with the devil, to gun down the man he asked so much of. It would only be one more turn of the page before he could find out what was in store for the rest of his evening. Driven to measures he'd never have believed only months ago, he sat planted against a T-post, bleeding into the dirt, reading some old book like a madman lost in the wilderness three weeks into a moonshine-fueled binge. He flipped the page one more time and allowed his eyes to hover over a new entry, each word more perilous than the last.

April 2, 1882

> *Tomorrow is the day. The Governor has promised a full pardon for my brother and I. He's promised my name to become a national hero. It's been months since we last exchanged words, but the deal remains the same. It's an eye for an eye, when it all comes down to it. I've done things no man should do, and I've seen things no man should see. If there are stories written about my name, I sure hope they don't know what I know. Redemption is a fool's promise. What I am after is something much more eternal. The plan is set, and the trap has been baited. A man of his stature surely sees when the world closes in around him in such a manner, but if he does not see me and my brother coming, it will be a miracle made by the grace of God. What comes for him is not justice, for a hand of mine could never enact such a thing on any other. What comes for him is pure hell-fire and brimstone, the souls of those he left in his wake. It may be by my hand, but it will be exacted by more wrong-doing than any man ever should in this wicked world. Fame and fortune and riches await my doing of this deed. These are the missing pieces to the life I want more than anything, and these are the things that will allow me to finally leave this life behind. It will be my escape. All I*

have to do is pull the trigger, because tomorrow is the day I kill Jesse James.

Bob.

"Fuck!"

Rob flipped frantically through the pages, almost tearing them from the journal as he practically begged for what would never be there. It was the last entry in the journal. There was nothing of use in the final words of Robert Ford, there was no hidden meaning or Nostradamus-inspired prediction of the future. There was nothing tangible he could dare to hope for. It was a history lesson, and more importantly, it was a waste of his time.

In a fit of anger, he slammed the journal into the ground and screamed with everything he had in him. He didn't care about what it had done for him, he only cared about what it could not do for him now.

He stared hopelessly into the trees, silhouetted only by the blackness of night, an endless depth to be lost in when reality was too much to bear. He stared on and on as the words of an auction against mankind itself came through the trees in the distance. The selling of women and children and dealers of death and destruction, made transactional by the four hooves and two horns he hand-delivered was enough to send him spiraling. Instead of fighting or running, he sank down and sobbed. There were no tears to stream down his cheeks, only the lonesome feelings that came with them. He was empty inside, without even the urge to run that had followed him for his entire life. He closed his eyes, finding little purpose in staring into the void above, and he decided to look into the one inside himself. Wallowing wasn't something he was used to, but there wasn't anyone or anything there to pull him out of it.

In his own drowning, Rob didn't realize the chants of *sold* from the would-be auctioneer, Mr. Woodson, had come to a stop. There was no rambling about cattle lots laced with double entendre, no cheers and applause to the tune of thousands of dollars. The auction chants had not been replaced by silence, though. Rob straightened his back and turned his head toward the bulk of the clamor pouring through the trees. It was difficult to make out at first. There were yells and demands being barked back and forth, and there was a thunder of what had to be hundreds of boots stomping through the woods as if men were scattering in every direction. He couldn't put the pieces together at first, but when the siren began blaring out into the night and the soft glow of red and blue finally disturbed the suffocating darkness, he realized the auction was being raided.

Just like the flipping of a switch, the law enforcement coming down on Mr. Woodson's big day changed everything for Rob. He could become lost in the fray, he could escape with the rest of the worst men the world had to offer, or he could even wait it all out and simply walk away as if nothing ever happened. Deep down, the urge to run away once again was building inside of his belly, and he knew, not everything was lost just yet.

The moment such a thought entered Rob's mind, he was nudged gently as if being touched by a hand that was not man's for the first time in his life. It was urging him to do exactly what he'd always wanted to do. With a reflection of red and blue light glinting off of the barbed wire tied around his wrists, he began working against their restraints, using his own blood to wiggle enough room to turn his hands. He listened to the shouts and screams and pleas of the bidders at the auction being raided, and he thought about those whose lives were being saved by the arrival of much-deserved justice. His eyes remained down through it all, focused intently on the wire keeping him from using his hands.

Another nudge pushed him harder. He could feel the urgency of fate weighing on him, whether it was his own death or the escape he had waited his entire life for. He pulled back against the barbed wire as hard as he could, hoping the blood would provide just enough lubrication to slip one hand free.

The nudge this time finally broke his concentration. It wasn't metaphorical or to be found only in his head, but it just about knocked him over to his side. When he finally allowed his eyes to lift, his heart pounded hard enough to burst through his chest. It was his American Paint, pushing his head harder and harder into Rob with its own sense of desperation. Tears filled Rob's eyes, and he stared in disbelief for just a few seconds.

The next pull of his hand sent it free through the barbed wire, despite slicing the back of his hand wide open before coming free. The blood flowed down his fingertips, making it difficult to grab the leather journal half buried in the dirt and the horn of the saddle when the paint kneeled down to make it easier for him to climb on top. His grip slipped at first, and he tumbled over onto the horse. The beast was as patient and understanding as Rob had experienced from any human in this world. He mustered just enough strength to try again and pulled himself up, screaming the entire time from blinding pain in his stomach. His wounds cracked and bled and burned with a ferocity he'd never experienced before. Adrenaline was the only thing keeping him moving.

If he was caught by the police in the middle of the woods so close to what was going on, he'd be guilty by association, and if they ever found out his name, he'd be guilty for a hell of a lot more than that.

The horse he'd come to trust with his life stood up like he'd never climbed into the saddle. It was effortless, and the trot that trusty old Paint broke into was as smooth as a Cadillac. He couldn't have been more grateful for anything in his life than that horse. The familiar bounce in the saddle was as warm of welcome as he could ever hope for, even if he felt every slight movement in the scrapes and cuts that looked like severe road rash covering most of the front of his torso.

Rob gripped the reins as tight as his fingers would let him and held onto the horn with the other hand, bracing himself from falling over at any moment. He focused on a single point a few feet ahead, then rode to it and repeated, over and over again, just to stay conscious in his escape. When he slipped, the horse's mane was there to grab and stop himself from sliding off either side of the saddle.

He wasn't sure how far he'd gone when the woods started to clear and the voices grew closer behind him. He was so focused on staying alive that he'd forgotten entirely about the possibility of coming across someone else in the woods. Whoever it was behind him was gaining quickly, and it forced Rob to heel the horse into more uncomfortable speeds. He bounced harder, grimacing every time he came down in the saddle.

A gunshot echoed through the trees behind him, and his chest tightened at the idea of a bullet finding his back after all he'd been through. All he could do was keep his head down low, keep trying not to fall off the back of the horse in pain, and find a way out of the mess he'd gotten himself into. It wasn't all that different from what he'd been doing for so long anyway. Running to spare his life was pretty much all he'd ever done, so he should have felt more than confident about what he was doing.

The only problem was something he couldn't explain, tugging at his heart, something telling him the worst was still yet to come.

Chapter 23

Tomorrow is the day.

The final entry of the journal Rob had read was only a brief bit of insight into the single moment that would come to define Robert Ford's life and the title of coward that was placed on his head from the moment he was born. It told of a man killing the very boss who promised a life he could not achieve on his own. It told of a man in over his head, forced into servitude against his own absurd dreams in a reality all his own.

Blackness had turned gray all around, signaling the coming dawn, the rising of the sun on a new day. Rob had found his second breath under duress, and he could only think about those four words from the final entry of the journal. If tomorrow meant anything, that meant it had to happen today. It would be a few hours before he'd see the glorious light of the sun and feel its warmth envelope all of him. It was difficult to understand why he wanted such a thing when his stomach seemed to be on fire, but he did.

A bullet whistled by and slammed into a tree no

more than five feet from where he was riding his Paint through the woods. Greenbriar whipped at his face as they picked up speed. Another bullet hit the ground in front of him, and dirt exploded into the air and into a cloud before he rode right through it. He thought about the revolver that was no longer tucked into his hip, and for about the hundredth time since he'd gotten back into the saddle of his horse, he wished it were where it belonged again.

Two bullets lodged into trees on either side of him only seconds after the yips and hollers of men he did not know cried out in the distance behind him. It was impossible to tell whether or not they were gaining on him, but Rob figured it best to just assume they were. His heels sank into the sides of the horse, and it tossed its head to the side before complying. The pain from the bouncing almost took his breath away, but another bullet screeched only inches beside his ear, and it left him unable to do anything but remain grateful for the breath still in his lungs.

All he wanted to do was keep riding. He didn't want to fight the cartel off or come forward to the law, he just wanted to leave. Bullets flew all around him, whispering through the brush or splintering trees in a thousand pieces, all as the Texas nighttime soundtrack was drowned out by sirens and screams in a flood of flashing lights.

Whether or not there was a lesson to be learned in the inescapable hell his own decisions had led him to was up to the judgment of someone smarter than him. The world would always turn as it always had. The people who exploit and those who are exploited will go around it, whether they want to or not. He was caught up in a cycle that was not of his own creation, and it was a fact of life that was impossible to ignore with everything going on behind him.

"You ain't goin' nowhere, you son of a bitch!"

The voice pierced Rob's entire existence and made the blood in his extremities boil as hot as the sun he was desperately waiting on to rise in the east. How could O'Kelley be on his tail after all that? There was no way he'd followed him this whole time. "I hate that jackass," he whispered to his Paint as they rode through the woods and into a brief clearing.

Bam. Bam. Bam.

The shots came from directly behind him. Each bullet blasting out like deadly warnings in the waning darkness, inescapable and inevitable, threatening what little hope Rob could still hold on to.

"I'm gonna take that scalp of yours," O'Kelley's voice was shrill. "You better keep runnin'!"

Bam. Bam. Bam.

The shots were closer this time. Rob clenched every muscle he had, right down to his ass cheeks. It felt like it would be a matter of time before one of those bullets landed in the middle of his spine and sent him tumbling from the back of the horse that'd just saved his life. He wanted to look back, to see if it was only the betrayer, or if there was a larger fight taking place that he wasn't even aware of. There was a sinking feeling deep in his gut that told him even a split second would cost him his life, though. He couldn't bring himself to risk it, so he just kept riding. He pushed the pain a little faster, despite his stomach feeling like it was gushing blood with every step.

"Got ya!"

The words came to Rob before he realized what happened. His first thoughts were how it was impossible for anyone to have closed the distance so quickly. All of that was dispelled when the rope slid down over his shoulders and inched its way down to his shredded and torn torso. "What the—" was all he could get out before the rope yanked him backward.

He shouldn't have been strong enough to hold onto the horn of his saddle. His American Paint shouldn't have been strong enough to withstand the sudden pressure, jerking him in the opposite direction he was sprinting in. For just a split second, Rob's face was pressed into the worn leather of his saddle being torn in two directions. His body threatened to give way, and he knew that'd be the end of everything he's ever known. The stars of Texas would no longer guide his path at night, and the shining sun would never blind him from where he should be. The cicadas would never buzz him to sleep again, and the crows' morning caws would never wake him earlier than he wanted. If he let go now, the only things he loved about life—and these days they seemed too few and far between— would be lost forever.

O'Kelley, if given the chance, would put more than one bullet through him. His life would be over, and there would be no more running. He couldn't let go. He was rag dolling around on top of the horse, and his situation was getting worse by the second. Something had to give. It would either be the rope, or his grip, and he only had control of one of those things. He held on tight. Before he realized what was happening, the rope began to slip from around his waist before breaking free and falling to the ground behind Rob and his horse.

It took everything he had to pull himself to safety while his paint continued sprinting through the woods.

The human body can endure far more than Rob understood at that moment. Everything hurt. There wasn't a single muscle in his body that didn't ache. The blood from his wounds had stained the horse, the saddle, what was left of his clothes, and even the reins he had a death grip on. It was everywhere he looked, and in the back of his mind, he wondered how long he'd have the strength to keep up with such torment.

The woods opened up just ahead of where they were running, and to Rob's surprise, a road ran right through where they were going. Mundane pavement and the passing droll of exhaust fumes pouring from vehicles flying by in either direction, contrasted his dire situation in an odd way. Rob saw headlights first, and his heart fluttered. It would be just what he needed to use as a deterrent to those trying to end his escape. If he could time the traffic just right, he could leave them all behind and find a new life for himself.

He just had to keep running.

When he made the edge of the road, he could hear indecipherable screams from O'Kelley closing the distance behind him. Vehicles rushing by did their best to drown out his threats, but they were still there regardless. Rob paid them no attention while he looked for oncoming cars on the two winding lanes with faded yellow and white stripes disappearing into the distance. A sedan sped by a second later, and Rob made his move.

Before the Paint he rode was able to put a single shoed hoof on the pavement, a pickup Rob could've sworn he recognized screeched to a stop just in front of where they were standing. There was a small gooseneck steel trailer hooked onto the truck, almost blocking Rob's view of who was driving.

"You gettin' in or what?" Sam shouted.

Rob didn't hesitate. He bailed from the top of his horse and flung the gate of the trailer open to push the American Paint inside. O'Kelley's menacing presence put a damper on their happy reunion in a hurry, though. All Rob could see was a pistol gleaming in the gray light of the coming dawn. It was like his name was etched into the barrel, and the bullet burning its way through what little rifling the four-inch barrel had could see only him.

In the blink of an eye, it ricocheted off the steel trailer where Rob and his horse were hidden in. Another bullet blasted out, this time from behind him.

"Go, dipshit!" Sam hollered in a frantic state, still squeezing the trigger to send cover fire at O'Kelley, hiding in the tree line.

The highway-side firefight lasted only a few seconds. The pops of gunshots did nothing to stop the traffic, and several people laid on their horns as they hauled ass around Sam's truck and trailer, halfway parked on the side of the road. Rob slid into the passenger seat, huffing and grunting in severe pain.

"I thought…" Rob forced out between gasps for air, "…you died."

"Me too," said Sam, who put his boot to the floor to send the truck roaring back onto the road to freedom. "I should've died back at the warehouse. When I didn't see you anywhere, I thought they'd already gotten to you. I thought it was a losing battle. So, I turned around and ran the same way we came in."

"That worked?"

"Well, other than this," Sam said, without moving his eyes from the road, and lifted his arm to show a heavily bandaged elbow and forearm on his right arm. "Bullet grazed me while I was runnin'."

"Take it from me," Rob answered, while lifting the torn remains of his shirt. "It could be worse."

The last Rob saw of Sam was a smile beginning to form on his face before two LED headlights, a mess of tangled steel, and shattered glass slammed into the driver's side of their pickup, traveling at unimaginable speeds. The collision sent Rob flying into the door panel, almost breaking his ribs, before the truck and trailer lifted up on one side and tumbled over into the ditch.

Rob listened upside down to the truck's horn drone on and on without end, until blackness overtook him and he drifted once more into the familiar embrace of unconsciousness.

Chapter 24

The sun's light, shining down its glorious rays on a new day, was what Rob saw when he finally opened his eyes.

The orange and yellow glow of a morning's dawn is, to most, a chance for a fresh start, a chance to tackle life's most difficult challenges, a chance to love, work, grieve, cheer, or pick yourself up again. There were so few souls on this planet who woke up to see the morning's light shining down on their face and were faced with the fact that it would be their last. Unfortunately for Rob, he was among those people.

His hands and arms were covered in shards of glass, digging into his skin. His knee was throbbing something awful, and his stomach, torn and shredded and bleeding, was painful enough to keep tears in his eyes through it all. His bottom lip was busted wide open, and one of his eyes was almost swollen shut. He wasn't sure if all of the blood staining what was left of his clothes and just about every square inch of his skin was his, but he was pretty sure most of it was. What little eyesight he had left was blurry and dazed. If his body could get any more distraught, he most likely wouldn't be alive to feel it.

His pain levels were no longer measurable on a one through ten scale. At this point, he was surprised he could even think to stay awake. He wanted nothing more than to drift off back into the warm, comforting darkness he'd just come from, but somewhere in the back of his head, he knew that'd be the last time he ever took a breath.

A grunt escaped his lips as he lifted his head to try and look around. Everything was a blur at first, but his eyes slowly focused and adjusted. He was sitting upright, as much as he could tell. His hands and feet were not bound, but he was uncertain if he could summon the strength to move them. When he realized he'd already pulled his hands up to his face and he could move his feet, he did the only thing that he could, the only thing he'd ever known—he ran.

Rob didn't get far, though. He barely even got to his feet before a fist almost the size of his head came down on him so hard he splayed onto the floor without a second thought. The back of his head suddenly hurt more than anything else on his body. All he could do was hold it in both of his hands and roll around in paralyzing pain.

"Don't do that again," a harsh voice came to his ears.

It was Dalton Woodson, the Bossman himself, standing above Rob and looking down at him like a man gazes at his steak dinner. There wasn't much fight left in Rob, but even when he was rolling around grunting and trying not to pass out from the pain, he knew a fight for his own life was about to ensue.

"Son of a bitch," Rob let out.

"You stay right there," Dalton said before turning to walk away.

Rob finally pulled himself back upright and propped up against an aluminum wall too dirty to show his reflection. He pushed his index and thumb into his eyes and tried to forget about just how much of his body hurt so desperately. He jammed his fingers harder into his eyes when the memories of what he'd just gone through started to return. He'd almost made it out. He'd almost escaped with what little life he had left in him, but someone collided with him.

Then he remembered Sam and his horse, and his head sank between his hands. There wasn't anything he could do to save them, and worse, he didn't even know if they were alive to save. He did know that if either of them were alive, they wouldn't be for long.

Rob lifted his head from his hands and finally looked around at where he was. It was four aluminum walls with two rows of eight-inch wide openings running the length of each wall, bordering all around him except for the front. There were shavings tossed haphazardly all throughout the floor, almost a foot thick, and the smell of manure and ammonia filled every breath Rob took in. He was in a cattle trailer. It was at least a twenty-four-foot aluminum gooseneck cattle trailer with both the back gate and the side ramp closed shut. He was alone, but not for long.

The side ramp slammed open, and the rush of night air with screeching cicadas filled the inside of the trailer. It was enough to make Rob wince, but when he saw Bossman dragging Sam by the scruff of his collar into the trailer, he couldn't bring himself to look away. Sam's eyes were filled with pain and regret. He was in need of an emergency room that would likely never come. Rob struggled to watch him get thrown face-first into the pine shavings filling the floor of the trailer.

"We're getting out of this, Sam," said Rob. It was all he could think of. He didn't quite believe it himself when the words escaped his lips, but when he saw a hint of something that could save both of their lives still wedged into his buddy's waistband, he perked up just a little. It was a snub-nose revolver, and if Rob played his cards right, it would be their ticket out of this mess. He started scheming in his head about how he could get his hands on that revolver, trying to force away the thoughts about why Sam wasn't going for it himself. If he was going to act, it would have to be now. "We aren't dying in this fuckin' trailer."

Bam.

A wet splatter hit Rob in the face before he knew what was happening. The gunshot left his ears ringing inside the aluminum trailer. He tried to focus on the gore in front of him, blood and brains and skull were everywhere. Still, he couldn't look away.

"No! You stupid son of a bitch! He didn't have to die!"

Dalton didn't say anything. He just raised the pistol that had taken Sam's life and aimed it at Rob. They stared at each other for a few seconds without so much as a whisper. Rob couldn't do anything but hope for each new breath that filled his lungs. Every second became one he didn't expect to have, and he only grew more grateful for what time he did have with each passing moment.

"That right there is where you're headed," Dalton finally spoke up. "Whether you die with a shred of dignity or not is the last choice you'll ever make in your life. I can guarantee that."

Rob spat what little he could muster up with his mouth dried and bloody. It was all the response he could give as he tried to process what was happening.

"You happy with how your life turned out? You took everything from me, and you couldn't even have the decency to show your face. You ran like a coward instead. A business built from the ground up, with my own two hands, was destroyed tonight and it was all because of you. Do you really think I can't build it again? When your brains are painted all over this trailer, I'm gonna walk out that door and do it all over again. Then, when all those crowds of people are cheerin' and markin' that beautiful little box with my name on the ballot I'm gonna take their power to make an empire twice the size of the one you burned down in one night. No one is even gonna remember your name.

Rob finally made eye contact with Dalton. He may have still been on his knees and struggling to breathe from the overwhelming pain coursing through his entire body, but for one of the first times in his life, he was ready to stand up for himself.

Tomorrow is the day.

The words echoed in his mind, and he believed every single one of them with every fiber of his being. They led him to stand up inside the trailer, to face down Dalton, and to speak his mind before it all came to an end.

"You think bein' a politician is gonna absolve you of what you done? Those women and children you sold to the richest cartel you could find are gonna do nothing but send you straight to hell, whether it's by my hand or someone else's."

"Maybe you aren't a coward after all," said Dalton, dropping the firearm to his side as he stared right through Rob. "Those people you think only come from south of the border are right here in our backyard, too. It ain't just the cartel. It's businessmen, community leaders, people you would never expect, who come to my auctions. How do you think I made enough connections to even try to run for office? They all want what only I can offer. I can get cowboys anywhere to run this ranch, and they'll bring enough cattle to supply anyone who wants a taste of what real freedom is. That's what this country was built on. Men who took what was theirs by any means necessary, men who were made into legend for crimes most would call unspeakable today. I ain't any different than them, and the people will love me dearly for it. You'll see."

"You can gun me down if you want, but I know what's comin' your way, and it ain't something you can ever escape," said Rob. Before he could finish speaking, he heard shuffling from just behind the trailer's rear exit. They were boots pushing into the mud they'd been parked in, unmistakable steps coming closer and closer. Rob felt his world closing in around him, and in what he considered to be his final minutes left on this miserable planet, he allowed himself to do the only thing he'd ever wanted for his entire life—escape.

His thoughts left the life-and-death situation he'd found himself in, the trailer he was being held captive in, and the unfortunate circumstances of his own birth that led him into such a mess. He may not have been able to run away, but he could, at the very least, escape into his own head and find a sense of peace he'd never been able to find in his life.

Instead of family and loved ones he'd left behind, money and possessions he'd gained, or fame and fortune he'd never have, his thoughts drifted back to the journal pulled from the old West. He thought of the words written by a coward, words which he placed his entire hope for survival into. He thought of his namesake, Robert Ford, and how he gunned down the infamous outlaw Jesse James with a single squeeze of his trigger, forever cementing each of their own places in the pages of history. He thought of what Jesse James did in his life and how a bullet he never saw coming made everyone forget the terrors he wrought. He thought of what Robert Ford was after, and how a single decision to gun down a man changed the course of history as much as his own life until the day he died. All it took was Jesse James turning his back on the man he never should have looked away from.

Then, as if guided by the hand of fate herself, that was exactly what Dalton D. Woodson did. He continued rambling as he looked away, talking of a future which only men as twisted as him could dream of, his name fueled into stardom and popularity by the most heinous acts any man could pull off. Rob felt that same touch of fate when he noticed the pistol Sam had failed to yank from his waistband had tumbled onto the floor of the trailer, no more than a couple of feet from where he was, buried in the shavings out of sight of the monologuing Bossman.

The next sequence of events was set in motion by something as mundane as a clattering of the trailer's back door. It swung open in a hurry, and Rob didn't hesitate. He knew what was happening before it could even come to pass.

It was O'Kelley who had slung the trailer door open, his pistol in hand, aimed right at Rob with deadly intent. O'Kelley squeezed the trigger just as Rob leaped to the ground.

Bam. Bam.

Two guns were fired. Two bodies hit the ground.

Lost in the ideation of a world long dead, never to return again, and an empire built on the graves of those most in need, catapulting him into influence and power, Dalton D. Woodson never saw the bullet coming. His stubborn life came to a not-so-stubborn end, drowned in red no different than the blood-stained on his hands when he collapsed down the ramp of the trailer and into the dirt below, his face buried in the mud and muck.

Bewilderment and confusion have a way of destroying a man's forged gaze of intensity. Lost were the determined focus and overly eager attitude in O'Kelley's face as he slowly realized what had just happened. Life drained from his eyes. A crimson hole began to grow in his chest, bigger and bigger, until blood drenched his sweat-stained shirt and his knees grew too weak to stand. He fell in an instant, staring endlessly into the void of night.

Rob was on his back, gripping the gun of his only friend in the world in both his hands, and aiming right where O'Kelley had fallen only seconds ago. His chest heaved up and down, and his finger remained clenched around the trigger until it turned red and purple. He couldn't move, or even blink, as he sat motionless, half buried in the shavings inside the trailer. With a sudden *thump*, he let his head fall back onto the floor, and the snub-nose revolver hit the shavings still grasped in his right hand.

He laid next to what remained of Sam and allowed himself to breathe, enjoying the air entering his lungs and the wind brushing against his cheeks. He was the only one still sucking oxygen, and after all the bullets had been fired, he struggled to believe he'd been caught in the middle of every single one of them, yet still came out alive. Sweat dripped down his head and into the shavings as he finally turned to see that even though Sam was missing half of his face, somehow his empty look was trained on Rob. There were no words to speak to a dead body. There was nothing that could be done. Rob just laid there. Then, without any reason, he started to croon:

> They call me a drifter, they say I'm no good,
> I'll never amount to a thing,
> Well I may be a drifter and I may be no good,
> There's joy in this song that I sing.

Time lost its meaning inside that aluminum trailer. There was nothing left, and most would be shocked to learn that some truths of the world remain so even in the presence of absolutely nothing. Rob could have done anything with his life, but freedom was his at long last, and there wasn't anyone left alive who could hold it against him. There was only one thing Rob truly wanted to do as he lay in the trailer surrounded by death—he wanted to run.

It was this very urge that pushed him to crawl to the ramp leading out of the side of the cattle trailer and stumble over Bossman's body to face the world as a man reborn, yet unchanged all the same. When he looked to his right, his heart damn near crawled out of his chest through his throat. A smile stretched across Rob's lips for the first time in what was no less than an eternity. His American Paint was standing there, waiting for him with an impatient look on his face, and a saddle already cinched around his back.

Rob didn't enjoy a single second of climbing on top of a horse that stood seventeen hands tall. When he finally got his ass in the saddle and the reins in his hand, he finally had a chance to run away from everything, to chase down the sunrise and start a new life, nothing like the one he'd led for so long. He reached into his back pocket and pulled out the small, worn black journal that had given him such an opportunity, and gave in to what he knew he had to do. Rob gently heeled the horse forward and patted him on the neck.

"We just gotta make one more stop."

Chapter 25

"It was in this room, I swear. It's around here somewhere."

"I already told you it's not here."

"It's not like it got up and walked away."

"You never listen, Davy."

"I'll find it."

"I don't see how you could find anything in this place."

"We don't exactly have an office, Rose. This is where *everything* ends up, one way or another."

"I'm just glad you ended up here."

"And I thought I was the romantic one," said Davy, turning to see the look on Rose's face he knew would be there. It never disappointed him, even after so many years together.

"Don't worry about it," said Rose. "It'll turn up when you least expect it."

Ding. Ding. Ding.

"Front alarm," Rose said, twisting to face the front door.

"Who the heck is coming out here this early in the morning?"

"I'll take over looking."

Davy took up Rose's offer without another word and walked through the old family home, lost out in the woods south of Caddo Lake like he'd been there for a dozen lifetimes already. He reached the front door and swung it wide open without even asking who was on the other side. He expected a salesman needing a check or a postman needing a signature, but when he saw what looked like a full-fledged cowboy standing in front of him, he couldn't help but crack a smile.

"My name is Robbie Ford, you can call me Rob," he said. Rob was wearing a wide-brimmed straw cowboy hat with a loose pearl snap tucked into starched denim pants that rested on a pair of ostrich leather boots and gold spurs still jingling. He held up the journal clutched in his hand and offered a gentle smile. "I have something that belongs to you."

"No shit?" Davy couldn't help himself.

"Who's there!" Rose called from the back room.

"I don't know who it is, but you'll never believe what he's got."

Rose poked her head out of the door before shuffling down the hallway with

an unexpectedly serious look on her face. She stood side by side with Davy before reaching out and snatching the journal from Rob's hand. She examined it for all of a few seconds before turning her attention to the cowboy in the doorway.

"Did you get what you needed out of it?"

Davy was immediately lost. He distorted his face and turned to look at Rose in the hopes of finding some reasoning behind her question.

Rob didn't miss a beat, though. "More than you know."

"Did you put the missing piece back?"

"As best I could," said Rob, looking down at the journal. "It belongs here with y'all."

"It does now," said Rose.

Rob turned to leave, but second-guessed himself halfway down the steps of the home and turned to look at Rose one last time. "How did you know?"

"It's history now," she said.

Rob smiled and walked back out into the yard, where his Paint was tied up. He swung his leg over the saddle and propped himself upright. He tipped the front of his hat at both Davy and Rose, standing in the doorway, and left the way he came in. His horse walked slowly at first, then sped up to a gentle trot before easing into a canter. By the time they'd reached the end of the dirt road, Rob and his horse were at a full gallop, kicking up dust into the rays of sun beaming down through the trees.

Rob was no longer running from an old life he couldn't escape—he was running toward a new one he couldn't wait to discover.

A Look at Book Two
THE FIGHTING EARPS

THE LEGACY OF A LAWMAN IS ABOUT TO BE TESTED.

The Holliday Ranch stands as the hard-fought heartbeat of Virgil and Angel's marriage. Born from the same bloodline of the legendary gunfighter Doc Holliday, one of the largest cattle ranches west of the Red River has become a historical landmark of hope, sweat, gunpowder, and grit—but it is on the verge of collapse. Debts are piling high, rustlers circle like wolves, and big money wants to buy them out—or burn them down trying.

When two strangers ride in, everything changes. One is Joe Clanton, offering a quick sale and an easy end. The other calls himself Wyatt Earp. Says he's chasing something buried in the dirt—something worth fighting for. Virgil doesn't trust either one, but Angel knows a battle's coming, and they'll need more than hope to win it.

As old bloodlines rise and long-dead feuds spark back to life, bullets fly and legends return to the dust. With his brother Morgan at his side, Wyatt steps into a war where justice doesn't wear a badge—and the past refuses to stay buried.

AVAILABLE FEBRUARY 2026

About the Author

Nicholas Osborn is a second-generation ranch owner and storyteller from the heart of deep East Texas. With a career encompassing everything from entertainment marketing to news journalism over the last decade, he has studied the craft of authentic storytelling and honed his writing throughout the years.

Nicholas's debut series aims to mythologize the pineywoods he grew up in and welcome readers to a new chapter of modern Westerns, born of the tall tales that helped shape the genre. His writing is inspired by the history of the Lone Star State, the greater United States, and the larger-than-life heroes, gunslingers, and "black hats" that gave us the myth of the west we know and love today.

Nicholas is an owner at his family's limousin cattle ranch and first-time father with his wife of over ten years. As one of multiple generations of his family working on the Red Rock Limousin Ranch, Nicholas has put his experience into words as an author with a passion to keep timeless Western culture alive and thriving for today's readers.

f ⓘ X